How to Build a
Stimulating and *Everlasting Love* in
Relationships

Felix O. Jeremiah

BALBOA.
PRESS
A DIVISION OF HAY HOUSE

Balboa Press books may be ordered through booksellers or by contacting:

Balboa Press
A Division of Hay House
1663 Liberty Drive
Bloomington, IN 47403
www.balboapress.com
1-(877) 407-4847

Because of the dynamic nature of the Internet, any web addresses or links contained in this book may have changed since publication and may no longer be valid. The views expressed in this work are solely those of the author and do not necessarily reflect the views of the publisher, and the publisher hereby disclaims any responsibility for them.

The author of this book does not dispense medical advice or prescribe the use of any technique as a form of treatment for physical, emotional, or medical problems without the advice of a physician, either directly or indirectly. The intent of the author is only to offer information of a general nature to help you in your quest for emotional and spiritual well-being. In the event you use any of the information in this book for yourself, which is your constitutional right, the author and the publisher assume no responsibility for your actions.

Any people depicted in stock imagery provided by Thinkstock are models, and such images are being used for illustrative purposes only. Certain stock imagery © Thinkstock.

Printed in the United States of America.

ISBN: 978-1-4525-7770-8 (sc)
ISBN: 978-1-4525-7772-2 (hc)
ISBN: 978-1-4525-7771-5 (e)

Library of Congress Control Number: 2013912432

Balboa Press rev. date: 8/7/2013
Bible verses from King James Bible

ACKNOWLEDGMENTS

HOW TO BUILD A STIMULATING AND EVERLASTING LOVE IN RELATIONSHIPS is about building a wonderful and selfless love in marriage relationships and to restoring that powerful love to dead relationships. This book is filled with a treasure of knowledge everyone in a relationship can learn and practice.

My special thanks go to the Almighty God who gave me life, health, and the knowledge to write this book. My thanks to Carmi D. Cabell, LICDC, who inspired me to write this book and helped to provide financial support needed in the project. My thanks also to Sister Ime Equere who supported me financially and provided the equipment I used for my work.

Finally, my thanks go to Mary Anne White, who devoted her time and love to edit this book.

I pray today that the Lord will support you and work with you in any project you undertake in this life, and that you will prosper in Jesus. Thank you and God bless you all. Amen.

CONTENTS

INTRODUCTION

In 2012, I was in a Courthouse (marriage section) in Columbus Ohio, with a very good friend of mine who was to marry his beloved fiancée. At one end of the court was a crowd that attracted my attention, so I asked someone who worked there what was happening? He looked at me and said, "That is the divorce section, I was shocked. Only a few people were in the marriage section, and what seemed like thousands of people waited for their turn at the divorce court. What is happening, Lord? My aching heart prayed. Turning to my friend, I said, "I hope you will not join the crowd in the divorce section someday, Tony. Tony said, "By His grace, I will not.

From that day my heart was heavily burdened. Why should people marry only to divorce? Why should they attempt it when they know that they cannot handle it? The Lord did not instruct us to marry and divorce. We vow to be married "till death do us part". My questioning led me to research why there is high rate of divorce. I discovered many ideas which you will read in this book. I started teaching what I discovered at our Bible study in the Church and discussed my discoveries with some professional counselors who actually led me to write this book.

It is quite true that knowledge is power, and what you do not know can cost or hurt you. Basic knowledge about love, relationship, and marriage would solve many problems we in co-habitation today; unfortunately, children do things on their own without having the knowledge needed to be successful in developing a love relationship. Too much liberty is anarchy and society devoid of a family unit along with co-habitation ethics, cause and create additional relationship problems. So knowledge is important, understanding is important, and the love of God is very important. We have to apply God's love, knowledge, and understanding to everything we do in life.

Marriage involves a lifetime of effort and patience. As a human being, you might find yourself falling into habits that can leave your spouse feeling distant and lonely. By breaking these habits and learning to understand your spouse, you will find that marriage will become less burdensome, and the feeling of love and commitment will be established. Marriage is not man's idea, it is God's idea. Anything God makes is perfectly good, so, if you fail in marriage, you did not fail because the marriage is bad. You fail because you did not develop your relationship according to the formula of the founder, who is God.

"And the Lord God said, "It is not good for the man to be alone. I will make a helper suitable for him." . . . So the Lord God caused the man to fall into a deep sleep; and while he was sleeping, He took one of the man's ribs and closed up the place with flesh. Then the Lord God made a woman from the rib He had taken out of the man, and he brought her to the man. The Bible says that the man was so happy, and recognized her as " this is the bone of my bones and flesh of my flesh" He called her 'woman' because she was made out of the man. Gen.2:18-22

PROBLEMS
IN
RELATIONSHIPS

Chapter 1
PROBLEMS IN RELATIONSHIPS

The marriage relationship was created to be the most united, most honored, most admirable, and respected union of human relationship to ever exist on earth. I strongly believe this is true. Love is the power that brings people together in peace. As the saying goes, "love makes every lion a pet". Love makes every difficult and dangerous person a friend. Indeed, love reconciles differences in people; love accommodates, tolerates, gives selfless services, and love shares with others.

Love gives birth to marriage; and marriage gives birth to a union of children and parents, which is known as a family, designed by God for the continuity of the world. Love, therefore, is a pro-life creator. Everything that God created is good and beautiful. Among them all, God cherishes the union between man and woman, and fellowships with them. God calls each marriage His family. Love is our connection to God and it cuts across all stages of human growth and development. We humans look at love and are mysteriously attracted to its nature. Only those who recognize it within themselves in their relationship with God are able to define love as "life". Love is life and it gives healthy life to your physical life. Love, in my own term is "an endless and selfless kindness one person extends to another person. It is not cruelty or wickedness one person extends to another, so a relationship that begins in love cannot turn to evil and destruction. The nature of love is always kind, simple, and transparent. Love makes every moment lively, hopeful, and interesting. These characteristics of love create an excellent condition for marriage, which then empowers creation of a family unit, which is often said to be representative of God's opinion that life should go on.

The subject of love and marriage is very important and all-inclusive because everyone that comes into this world is directly involved. Whether rich or poor, black or white, royal or subject, you must know that every love and marriage relationship has its do's and don'ts. Together, they make a vital and profitable relationship but one without the other causes grief and pain. Let us look at it another way. Have you ever sat down to ponder how and why people fall in love? This is a mystery. It is beyond chemical attraction. Men talk about the existence and life of love, but not love's conception and birth. Most people out of ignorance, or half-knowledge, do say that "love is blind," but to me, this blindness, or lack of vision and foresight is the genesis of all the broken love relationships and divorces that have become a tradition of our society.

How can love be blind where it sees attraction, and beauty? Love is not blind. People fail to see that love is beyond their temporary vision. Love is not temporary attraction. Anything temporary fades and dies but love is everlasting, Love never dies. Loves grieves to see people failing to it – and how people suffer as a result. Falling in love and going into marriage is not and should not be considered child's play. Maturity is essential to a love relationship, and you have to think and consider and study a relationship with both physical and spiritual eyes open. Your senses must be very alert and your knowledge about what the relationship means to you must be very acute. Love and marriage is the business of your heart. There is no glory or honor in divorces and break-ups. Broken hearts are hard to mend; hearts must be handled properly with His divine laws and knowledge. Every faulty love or marriage relationship is aggressively hurtful, and devastating to the individuals involved and to the society in which they live. Understanding the ethics of relationships is more profitable than that of sex education which so many schools have included into their school curriculum. Instead they should teach love which prompts sex. Any sex relationship done outside love ends in chaos and in a bitter experience to young lovers.

A real love and marriage relationship is a wonderful and sweet union. Two members of opposite sex, each of whom have a relationship with God, join in total agreement to build and design a wonderful law-abiding part of the society and contribute immensely to the peaceful co-existence of the world for the rest of their lives. The problem of broken homes, break-ups and divorces was not like this in the beginning. We have thrown away divine laws, traditions, and every element of cultural unity that upholds the pillar of love and marriage. We have fallen apart. Look around you and tell me, what do you see? I see single mothers, divorcees, street-children, able bodied people in the shelters, and widows and widowers, who have murdered their spouses as result of ugly and complicated love relationship. Yes, these are what I see and all are by-products of broken homes, broken relationships, and divorces.

Every one of us has wandered very far from God as a result of the liberty we want for ourselves. As a consequence, we have created this anarchy in relationship for generation yet unborn.

A diminishing crisis can be managed, and hopefully come to an end someday. But a raging crisis cannot. This poses a threat like a time-bomb in our society. The upcoming generations who know nothing about pure and godly love relationships and marriages will all their life live in danger. A child who is taught sex education, for example, knows only about one thing. It is sex: how to sex, how to protect oneself from diseases and pregnancies, and perhaps the right age to begin to sex. It is good but partial knowledge - not the sum. The child does not know who to sex, so the present generation sexes anything: animals, reptiles, birds, and same-sex individuals. Why they must sex with whoever they want to is not even known to them. They don't know love that breeds sex, but just sex for the sake of sex. Love now becomes the product of sex rather than sex being the product of love. This is the second genesis of the problem of broken homes and divorces in our society.

Every grown-up person was once a child and children learn by watching, listening, and experimenting. Most couples are so careless and immoral that their own children, or children around them, become like them. There are many things children should not see until they grow up, because once seen is forever known.

RELATIONSHIP PROBLEMS ARE UNIVERSAL

One interesting thing about love and marriage relationship problems is that it is universal. Kings and queens, presidents of great nations and poor nations alike are in relationships. Heads of religious organizations and their followers, rich people and poor people are all living with this problem. Children born today anywhere in the world will grow to inherit the problem. This problem needs a solution

When I was in Africa, I saw the problems of relationships but it was not so exposed. African culture, church and mosque make divorce evil and secret, although it is ongoing secretly across that society. Africans are poor, and we know that love without money never lasts long, but older people in African villages, they have no money and no splendor life, and yet their relationships with their spouses are sweet and highly coordinated. The few rich people who I thought would live happier, safer, and more united with their spouses are even worse, and those who teach the word of God also struggle with relationship problems. I concluded that the problem is something more than poverty. They are wandering away from God and tradition.

I wanted to know more. I thought the people of Asia would have better relationships, but I saw many complicated problems of love and marriage relationships. People struggled to stay in love and people were crying "foul" and checking out of relationships. Broken homes and broken relationships were normal ways of life. If the problem was caused by over-population, many people were looking for cheap sex. This is hard to answer, too. Some people I interviewed said they would choose to remain single rather than going into a relationship that would break their hearts. Nobody is ready to love for love. In Europe, people often commit suicide because of being involved in a bad relationship. Why can't people with good living standards maintain their relationships in a decent loving manner?

America! God's own country! 'Heaven on Earth nation? God have mercy! This is the worst nation on the surface of the Earth, for a love relationship. Why is America in this huge mess regarding relationships? Why are almost 75% of the American adult populations divorced? Why are great numbers of American people living as single parents? Are same-sex relationships the result of frustration and heartbreak caused by broken relationships with the opposite sex? So many broken homes in American society leave innocent children devastated in project housing, public shelters, and places of lawlessness and crime. No wonder there are so much crime in American society. Children beget children, because they have received no knowledge about the value of relationships. Children want someone to love them and want them – so they create babies for themselves in great ignorance. Children need to be shown that they have the right to good parenting which will, in turn, supply a good education, good healthcare, and a good home life. Children need good guidance to grow to be good citizens – this is true of any nation. Without good parenting, children will not learn or develop a sense of responsibility. Without responsibility children cannot make good decisions. Without the ability to make good decisions, they will live their adult life in misery and danger. The only right that will be known as a child is the right to live a good life.

Felix O. Jeremiah

THE UNDENIABLE URGE IN RELATIONSHIP

Love and marriage relationships are the urges you cannot ignore or deny when an individual is of age. Relationship is not an act and cannot be acquired by wealth or might but by natural disposition by God in every normal human being. Denying those urges, as a grown up, and normal individual results in activities that will never be good and appreciable life-style in any good society.

COUNSELORS OF LOVE RELATIONSHIPS AND MARRIAGES

These global situations of ugly relationships problems have prompted many colleges and universities to create a curriculum of counseling or psychology, yet the problems grow worse by the day. Many of the counselors and psychologists themselves are victims of poor relationships and divorces too. Some of their children are also now wayward and live in the streets. This is why every one of us needs God in our relationship and also believe God to lead you to a good counselor who is great in his or her relationship. The job of counseling is not an easy one, because a piece of advice that is not properly applied can destroy a relationship completely. I pray relationship counselors and encourage them to do great jobs, but put their trust in God for better wisdom.

Love concept was instituted by the Creator, with a natural procedure of attaining it, but man has changed God's procedure to using human wisdom and approaches to love. Human ways fail all the time, we cannot even manage our one-to-one relationship as humans, how much more of possibly managing and leading our society right.

Love cannot be stopped. Love is the nature of man created in the divine image, and love is what will heal the world. This foundation has been laid down from the beginning of the world. The only way to solve the problems of relationship is to seek a way to make relationships work, and this is exactly what this book is all about.

No retreat or surrender in love and relationships is possible. Until a way to make love work, create a sweet relationship is found, we will continue to seek a solution. Divorce is never a solution; a break-up is never a solution. Divorce multiplies the problem that is destroying our children and society today. In the beginning, divorce was not an option. Divorce was a source of shame and pain. Our forefathers had love relationships and marriages that ended in death. If the present is not working, perhaps we should look at the past to learn how to handle relationships in happiness and unity.

Relying on the current education and knowledge is a detour in the divine plan for relationships. All attempts to go further lead to destruction. The earlier we realize this will be better for us and for our generations yet to be born. So many individuals and families have lamented the agony they go through daily as a result of divorce and broken relationships. "This is a time bomb," someone said to me. If the rate of divorce and broken relationships is not checked soon, the devastation to society will be huge.

SOME PAINFUL EFFECTS OF BROKEN LOVE RELATIONSHIPS AND DIVORCES

Divorce and broken relationships have had adverse effects on society. Every area of the family unit is harshly affected. Let's consider some of these effects.

Effect of Divorce on Children:

Children are dangerously affected by divorce. First, children lose the relationship between them and their parents when the parents are divorced. The children begin to lack home training, practical support, financial support, and most of all- love. Emotionally, these children become depressed, wayward, arrogant, and lawless. Children of a divorced couple are less cultured, feel a sense of early responsibility or guilt, and lack the ability to handle conflicts. Children are thrown into immature situations which they lack social skills and know-how to handle. These children confuse love and sex. Children from divorced homes face the danger of early pregnancies and child-rearing, and their attitude toward marriage is destructive. These children often have no incentive for continued education, so they lose interest in school and skill training. They struggle financially throughout their life.

Single parenthood has much great knowledge missing in it; most importantly, genuine love. Waywardness in single parenting is high and often causes one to be a school dropout, and engage in juvenile delinquency. Some children become hardened criminals who frustrate law and order, and kill people. Some children end up hating both parents and resolve to kill them, or join gangs to create security and the sense of belonging in society. Some children became depressed and deteriorate in health. Some even commit suicide.

Children who up in an intact family with both biological parents present, do better on wide range of outcome. They are more peaceful, cultured, loving and balanced in thoughts and deeds than children who grow up in a single parent family.

Effects of Divorce on Spouses

There are numerous effects of divorce on spouses. Both spouses are emotionally depressed, especially when they can no longer share quality time with their children. Financially, spouses are affected by attorney fees, renting a new home, and caring for their children living elsewhere. Spouses sometime become alcoholic or end up taking drugs to cope with the situation. Some spouses become wretched from paying child support to their ex-spouse and hate life. Spouses can end up in shelters when they cannot afford to pay rents; some become harlots and expose themselves to dangers of being killed by addicts and robbers. Some spouses psychologically become sick and die; or commit murder or suicide.

Effects of Divorce on Society

Divorce is a poison and a threat to a society. Some children of divorced couples do get involved in criminal activities that deprive good people of their money and privacy; they commit fraud, fight, and kill people. These are some of the negative effects of divorce on society. Religious practices weaken; interest and comfort in education diminish. Divorces increase crimes such as, sexual abuse, use and sale of drugs, and other broken laws. While government spends more money combating crime, the society lives in fear.

THE FOUNDATION OF DIVORCES AND BROKEN HOMES IN OUR SOCIETY

Chapter 2
FOUNDATION OF HOMES AND ENVIRONMENT

Everything on earth, whether physical or spiritual, or any other area your mind may explore has a beginning, and that very beginning is called the foundation. The foundation is, by and large, a structure which is laid for us to build upon. The foundation cuts across every sphere of human life and development. If positively laid, it breeds success in human endeavor. If it is negatively laid, it multiplies failure, pains, and misery in human striving. We cannot build anything without laying a foundation. Foundation is like the first milk fed into a child's sub-conscious mind for life endeavor. A good and positive foundation allows achievement with little effort. On the other hand, a negative foundation offers little or no success. History has shown that the laying of a negative foundation seldom builds a positive destiny. People must combine hard work and expend great spiritual energy to change a negative foundation into a positive one on which they can build.

Foundation is a critical factor in our lives. In this book, we look at foundation in every area and how it positively or negatively affects the life we live, the way we think, the way we behave, and also the way we handle situations.

Felix O. Jeremiah

HOMES AND ENVIRONMENT

In every person's life, the home in which he/she is born has much to do with his/her success or failure on earth. This is followed by the environment in which he/she grows. Home is the beginning of everything we know, feel, act upon, and believe. A home is made up of father and mother who lead and teach the basic things of life. Brothers and sisters are like mates but are blood connection in nature and learn from the parents. A home could also include grandparents who are great mentors. Uncles and aunts contribute as well, but the most important thing is how they relate to each other. In the earlier ages when people lived in tribal families, this home set-up had much impact in every child's life and development. Today the opposite is true. Civilization has torn us apart and relationship is no longer what it used to be. Everybody now minds his or her own business, and lives wherever they choose. The home setting has shrunk to be just husband, wife, and children only. This limits the home and the relationship therein.

In a home, the father is the head. He must be a man of wisdom, knowledge, and understanding. He must know what he believes in and what his focus is for the family. He gives instructions and expects those instructions to be carried out. He must spend time with his family, teaching his child or children about life issues: what is right and what is wrong, and directing them into their destiny. He must be there to teach them humility and spirituality: he must be there to demonstrate love and care. He must be there to teach them how to live and relate with others, observe actions and reactions and challenges. A father must have self-esteem and impart that to his children. He must always show his children the God he serves and believes in and encourage his children to be good and responsible citizens. A father must not abuse or fight with or beat his wife. In the home, every matter of disagreement must be discussed and settled in the bedroom at bed time. He must make sure that love and happiness reign in the home and be a provider for the home.

In a home, a mother is the second in command. She must acknowledge that she is not the head of the house but the head of the children. The idea of equal partnership, 50/50 must not exist between husband and wife. This idea is destructive and from the mouth of Satan. A woman and a man can never be equal. In the beginning, God made man the head and the provider of the home and so shall it be to the end. A mother must know that and have a great deal of respect and honor for her husband. She must give the instructions of her husband to the children, and the children must fear and honor their father in love. A mother must not be a nag and argumentative. She must not molest her husband in any manner or form before the children. A mother must keep God-fearing friends and must be present for her children, teaching them to be good and responsible people in the society. She must make sure that there is always love and happiness in the home.

If father and mother do not provide this foundation for their children, then the children will learn in the street what will destroy them. There is no man, no teacher out there, who will teach your children better than you how to be useful to society. If you do not do it, do not blame the child. Blame yourself for doing nothing for your children. As a result, they will definitely be nothing to you.

Our society today values the drive to achieve and live a great life; to be a man and woman of society. Fathers are not at home, mothers are working and children are left alone with pets in the home. Consequently, pets and children have better relationships than parent and child. In some homes, the children are left with house maids or nannies that do not care what the children become. Some nannies even abuse the children sexually and corrupt their minds even before they grow. Some initiate children into witchcraft and occultism. If our homes are not guided by fathers and mothers, enemies will guide them for us. Home is one of the greatest foundations that mold a man for great achievement while alive on earth.

Environment is as important as our homes. Environment affects our growth, our character, our ideas and beliefs. These are basic elements of human development and achievement. Many children today are brought up in areas of crime and violence, where beating and raping of women occurs, as well as selling and using drugs, robbing and picking pockets; and many other crime and evil acts occur. These acts are what all children within the environment see and know, so they think that is just the way life is. Now, we ask ourselves: How can someone brought up in this way live a good life and be responsible in a marriage? The answer is: It is not possible. A good and decent environment adds value to the life of a person anywhere in the world, and it is the responsibility of parents to determine where and how their children are raised. If parents are careless, their children future will be damaged. The future is a result of decisions one makes each day.

I also see some communities in different countries where people live closely, like families but they are not blood relatives. In many countries, men, women, and children live together in an indecent manner. They share food, clothes, and sex together without shame. Men change sex partners like clothes, and women sleep with their friend's sex partners with ease and pride. This kind of place corrupts children quickly and easily. People brought up in this kind of environment never live in marriage relationships successfully. They have no importance attached to morality and responsibility. Environment is an issue to be considered critically when raising children.

Most young people are raised in communities where husbands and wives fight, curse, and even go to police for relationship issues, and most of the youth live their lives that same way for life. Some environments are so rotten that everything you see daily is immoral. Once children are engaged in immorality, they never do well or concentrate in any meaningful endeavor in life again, No man combines pleasure and labor together and makes headway. Life must be given meaning in a good home with a healthy, stable environment. The mind of a child absorbs much and what it records can never be wiped out. One should always work with the mind along his or her life journey.

If you want happiness for yourself and your children, you must organize your home and make it a place of moral decency, mutual respect, and ethical responsibility. A home should be a place where the husband and wife live in love and harmony, a place where there are rules and love of God; a place where children depend on their parents for wisdom, knowledge, and understanding, and a place where people know how to appreciate one another. When every member of a home cares for each other and understands the pride of morality, the home becomes a place where family members believe in and share labor and integrity. It becomes a place where a father's presence guides his children to excellence, and a place where children never have to claim that they have rights because they understand love, obedience, and unity.

Like a home, an environment (neighborhood) should be where decent and responsible people live. An environment is where men of purpose live, as role models in the society. Great mentors and hard-working people live within the society, and couples live in love and peace. An environment that hold morality in high esteems, everyone is his brother's keeper. This kind of environment produces great men and women in any society.

EVERY INDIVIDUAL NEEDS A HOME

Charity begins at home. Knowledge, wisdom, and responsibility begin at home. Birds have nests to call home; foxes have holes that they call home. Every living being has a place to begin their day and a place to retire at its end. There is a big difference between someone raised in a home and one raised in a house. Home is comprised of a father, a mother, and children surrounded by a community comprised of culture, rules and order. A home is a place of behavioral decency.

Children who grow up in a home are easily known. They grow

healthy and have peace and happiness in their life. They are more respectful and obedient to rules and regulations in any institution, they are more confident in anything they do and enjoy their youthful exuberances. Children learn by watching what others do, so children that grow in a home learn good things that will catapult them better future and they make quality relationships. Our society will be more peaceful and enjoyable if every member of the society belongs to a home. Home gives individual more focus and composition for the future. Parents must do their best make a home for their children and they will be proud for such venture in future.

Disadvantages of been raised outside the home

The children who were ignored at home or who lived in bad households have trouble expressing themselves verbally. They live in fear and don't believe in their selves. These class of children are quick to anger and live violently; they don't know love and have no happiness and joy as children. They don't do well in school and find it difficult to associate with others. They also have trouble with social skills. Sharing and cooperating is difficult for them, and they had trouble playing mates. Children raised in a house live in bitterness and hardly make any quality decision, their future are always cloudy and they never succeed in any relationship. This is not their fault but their parents who failed to make a home and raise them there.

How to know children from troubled homes and bad parenting?

The effects of bad parenting and child-stress can be seen when children fall behind their peers in school. Children who have trouble communicating with their teachers and peers, they have anger and quick cry, and they have difficulty in school home work. They don't pay attention or concentrate in school. They have frustration looks all the time and have no interest in school. They are always involved in fight as a means of defense, and they don't have love.

Criminal Activities in early life

Children brought up in a bad home and bad parents end up being school dropouts and live in the street. These children grow up to be nobody and cannot be gainfully employed, they likely to turn to illegal activities and end up with a criminal record. The fact that the person has a record makes it harder to find work after serving a sentence, which leads to more criminal activities, and the whole thing turns into a vicious cycle. Many of them join gangs for protection and sense of belonging in a society. Some become rapist and different evil characters in a society. Nobody is born with a criminal spirit in him; it is acquired from bad parenting, homes, and environment.

Addiction Issues

Children from bad homes and environment become drug, alcohol, and sex addicts due to their constant search for stress relief, happiness and confidence. They become addicted as they use they every day to find result. Some also became addict through their addicted parents and role model in their environment. Others become addict through selling it make a living. Orange tree can never bear lime, good homes and environment cannot produce a criminal, and every parent should know that homes and environment have much to do in a child's future.

Chapter 3
ASSOCIATES AND LIFE STYLE

Associate means joining to one other or others as partners, friends, or companions and doing things and living life in common. Lifestyle is a kind of pattern one has adopted for living his or her life. This adopted pattern could be through personal introduction, copying from a personal model, imitation, or through mentoring: all have an impact in one's earthly life. The saying "Show me your friend and I will tell you who you are," is a true statement of fact. My father used to tell me, "When a goat befriends a dog, it eats feces." A relationship with immoral mind corrupts good character.

Let us look at what the book of law and life says about the company we keep.

THE HOLY BIBLE

> "But now I am writing to you, do not associate with anyone who bears the name of brother if he is guilty of sexual immorality or greed or is an idolater, reviler, drunkard or a swindler. Do not even eat with such a person." I Cor. 5:22 (KVJ)

> "Do not be deceived, bad company ruins good morals." 1Cor.15:33 (KJV)

"Whoever walks with the wise becomes wise but the companion of fools will suffer harm."Prov.13:20 (KJV)

"Leave the presence of a fool, for there you do not meet words of knowledge." Prov. 14:7 (KJV)

"Blessed is the man who walks not in the counsel nor stands in the way of sinners, nor sits in the seats of scoffers but his delight is in the law of the Lord and on His law he meditates day and night. He is like a tree planted by streams of water that yields its fruits in its season and its leaf does not wither. In all that he does, he prospers. The wicked are not so, but are like chaff that the wind drives away." Ps.1:1-4 (KJV)

"I do not sit with men of falsehood, nor do I consort with hypocrites. I hate the assembly of evildoers and I will not sit with the wicked." Ps.26:4-5 (KJV)

I Corinthians 15:33 in the KJV states "Be not deceived: evil Communications corrupt good manners. The scripture concerns our associations and the impact on the life we choose to live. The effect is very clear as written; it cannot be manipulated in any way, no matter what translation you read. Take a look at the same verse of scripture, (I Cor. 15:33), from various translations of the Bible:

BIBLE TRANSLATION

"Do not be misled: Bad company corrupts good character" New American Standard. Bible (2007)

"Stop being deceived: "Wicked friends lead to evil ends." (KJV Cambridge Ed.)

"Be not deceived: evil communications corrupt good manners". Aramaic Bible in Plain English

"Be not deceived, evil discourse corrupts pleasant minds". God's word Translation

"Don't let anyone deceive you. Associating with bad people will ruin decent people". King James Version

"Be not deceived: evil companions corrupt good morals." American King James Version

"Be not deceived: evil communications corrupt good manners." American Standard Version

"Be not deceived: Evil companionships corrupt good morals". Douay-Rheims Bible

"Be not seduced: Evil communications corrupt good manners." Darby Bible Translation

"Be not deceived: evil communications corrupt good manners." "English Revised Version"

"Be not deceived: Evil company doth corrupt good manners". Webster's Bible Translation

"Be not deceived: Evil communications corrupt good manners". Weymouth New Testament

"Do not deceive yourselves: Evil companionships corrupt good morals." World English Bible

"Don't be deceived; Evil companionships corrupt good morals." Young's Literal Translation

"Be not led astray; evil communications corrupt good manners."

No man is an island; we live in a society that is complex and surrounded by all kind of people. We might also have people in our lives who do not know dignity; all it takes is "firm" stand that you will not allow anybody to corrupt your mind. This is an era of Television shows and movies that tend to weaken our belief values and moral, parents must be strong and strict to keep their children off from such places and activities. Parents should make some home laws that will protect their children for the future and also be role model to their children.

Apostle Paul in the Bible said: "Even though we are surrounded by unbelief, we must not be misled." Parents have to guard their children's hearts from allowing bad company and social net works to corrupt their good training. Send them to where they can be uplifted spiritually and as the word of God is grounded in them, their lives will remain focused in things that profit.

THE HOLY QURAN

Al-Ahqaaf 48:13-14 "Verily those who say our Lord is only Allah and thereafter stood firm and straight on them shall be no fear nor shall they grieve. Such shall be the dwellers of paradise, abiding therein (forever) a reward for what they used to do" (Ali 2011)

Al-Kahf 18:28 "And obey not him whose heart we have made heedless of our remembrance, one who follows his own lust and whose affairs have been lost."(Ali 2011)

Al-Zukhurf 43:62 "Friend in that day (the Day of Judgment) will be foes except muttaqoon." (Ali 2011)

Abdullah ibnMasood "Nothing tells about anything more than a mantels about his companion." (Ali 2011)

Al-Haafi zibnHajar "There is in this hadith prohibition of keeping the company of those who can harm one in religion and worldly matters and an encouragement for keeping the company of those who benefit in this matters." (Ali 2011)

The Shaykh- rahimahullaah "Know O pious brother - may Allah make our affairs Good- that the manners of companionship and good relationships are of various types, of which I will explain, such as will show the person of intellect the manners of the Believers and the Pious; and come to know that Allah the Most Perfect, the

Most High has made them a mercy and helpers towards each other, which is why the Messenger of Allah (saws) said, "The example of the Believers, in their mutual love and mercy is like the example of a body, if one part feels pain, then all of the body suffers in sleeplessness and fever."(Ali 2011)

And he (saws) said, "The Believer to the Believer is like a solid building, one part supporting the other." [4] The Prophet (saws) also said, "the souls are arrayed armies, so those who knew each one another before, will be friendly..." [5] So if Allah intends good for His servants, He grants them companionship of the people of the Sunnah, righteousness and adherence to the Religion; and keeps him free from the companionship of the people of innovations. The Prophet (saws) said, "A person is upon the religion of his friend, so let every one of you look to whom he keeps as a friend."

To associate is human nature; no matter who a man is, he must have friends and allies. Satan itself has its own friends. No one stops anyone from keeping a friend, but our parents are correct to stop us from keeping bad friends or companions. The company adults keep influences them and that is why some good people become evil: becoming alcoholics, womanizers, clubbers, cheats, and deceitful. Some women, through their friendships become abusive, flirts, disobedient, quarrelsome, nags, cheats, and disregard their husbands. These are influences from the associates with whom we surround ourselves. If this can happen to adults who know what they want in life, who have a sense of humor, who have acquired experience as to what life is all about and still choose to disorganize their life, imagine how much more a child can be easily carried away by the tricks and pleasures of false friends and associates. The company we keep and the lifestyle we choose

to live have a great impact on the life one on earth lives. Relationships influence and lifestyle are distinguishing factors that can either make or break a person in life.

Conclusion

Many people are dead, may are in the hospital, and many are in jail because of the bad company they keep. You might think you are very strong in your mind and no one can lead to do bad thing, but watching them would someday influence you to become a part of their action. The only good thing here is to keep off and befriend great people and you will become great.

Chapter 4
RELIGION AND BELIEFS

There are so many religions on earth today and most of them teach about the fatherhood of God and the brotherhood of mankind. In these you will learn something like the relationship between God and man, the relationship between man and man and the relationship between man and the universe. Every one of these relationships has great effect on one's behavior and life on earth. It does not matter where you are, as long as you understand the "Do's and Don'ts" of the life teachings that make one a peaceful, law-abiding citizen of any society, with a future full of hope and treasure on earth.

It is imperative that a society be involved in some discovered spirituality because any society that does not recognize God and Love amongst man is a great mess. Matters of faith, religion, and belief vary greatly in the hearts of the people all over the world. Religion deals with the family setting of the people, with the ideas that transcend everyday living. People of a particular religion are coordinated and joined perfectly together because of their doctrine. Religion is a matter of faith; religion encourages people to look hopefully to a better life to come on earth and life after death. There are differences that exist between religious beliefs and societal lives and religious beliefs teach how to disengage from many activities which the society endorses.

In religion, there are so many things that are referred to as taboo. Practitioners are cursed if they are involved with them. Parents disown their children who are involved in those taboos and spouses are forced to separate or divorce if one of them is involved.

In his book, Karl Marx on Religion, Marx declared that religion served ruling elites by legitimizing the status-quo and diverting people's attention from the social inequities of society. In other word, religion should not be a gathering to praise, admire and worship leaders but to re-address and rebuild the society for morality and godliness (Marx, 2002).

In Peter Berger and the Study of Religion, Linda Woodhead viewed religion as a social construction, placing everyday life under a "sacred canopy" of meaning. These sociologists agree that religion has a major importance for consideration by individuals in society (Woodhead, 2001).

From childhood to adulthood, the life we live has stages; and every stage offers decisions that influence one's future and actions.

Children are very intelligent people who learn by observing. What they see is what they desire to imitate. Without religious beliefs and moral deeds, the children grow ill along with the society.

Adolescents fare even worse, during the period of realization of self, when there are various social and personality developments. Adolescents experience increased interactions with opposite-sex peers and attention is devoted to identity formation and adoption of the lifestyle of people they cherish. Adolescents ask questions such as, "Who am I, who do I love to look like and what do I want to accomplish in my life?" The only thing that checks all that the society offers is spiritual beliefs, so when there is no religion, the adolescents fly with the worldly deeds of the society.

Adolescence is also a time when everything in life is questioned, including culture and religion. It is the time when everything in life influences adolescents- television, music, movies, and the Internet-

sot it is hard to believe that religion can make that much difference. Adolescents have parents and government to control them and teach them how to live their lives before they become adults. Adolescents are often seen as challenging in society and they are the upcoming future leaders of any society. Adolescents take on activities considered to be immoral, including sexual behavior, and delinquent activities, including violence. They must be constantly and closely checked and taught the way of future excellence.

Adolescents thought processes change as well. An adolescent may think that he or she is in this world alone and no one else can understand what they are going through. This is where teaching of religious beliefs can address most of the issues they have that they do not want to share with anyone. When an adolescent has no faith, he or she is all alone and could spend all his or her life on the wrong road. This is also dangerous for society.

When we emphasis on religion to people, some carless parents question - what is it about religion that makes a difference in the life of a man? Religion reinforces messages about working hard and staying out of trouble, behavior toward sex and the ethics of marriage and orientation toward a positive future and eternity.

Religion is a global phenomenon that has taken part in all human culture. It is an aspect of experience that can traverse, include, or exceed other parts of life and society. How society is structured has a profound impact on the decisions that adolescents make. How the parents raise the child is crucial to their decision-making. The extent of the teen's religiosity is important. Not only is it a part of a person's life, but also of group development. Religion can be organized and expressive and include patterns of behavior, as well as patterns of language, thought and idea.

Remove religion and beliefs from the life of an individual, then he or she becomes a domestic beast whose actions cannot be predicted at any time.

The adult stage of life is one where all that one should be is fixed. This is the stage where an adult is respected or disrespected, the stage where you can call the life of a man by its name. At this stage, one either influences a society or succumbs to the society. Religious beliefs are the only power through which people reform with ease and submission.

Religion can be a sensitive subject for some, especially if you and your spouse do not share the same belief system. While not sharing the same religion doesn't condemn a marriage to failure, sharing the same belief is a large part of successful marriages. Many marriages of mixed faith do wonderfully well, but it can sometimes be a hard road learning how to respect each other's different belief systems. Looking into it, many different religions teach that it is not wise to marry someone of a different faith or one who does not believe the same things you do. If you look at it, couples that have different faiths and are both strong in their religious values might just be inviting controversy into their home.

Living your religion can sometimes mean cultural differences. There are many traditions that one religion might follow that another one does not. How will you raise your children? What traditions will you take from each other's belief system and how might it affect your children? If these questions are answered well in advance, there will be less tension later on. If your philosophy in matters of religion does not allow you to respect the beliefs of your partner, then you will have problems. For a lot of people, religion is the cornerstone of their core values, and if you cannot respect each other's ideas of religion, then problems will most definitely arise.

Ultimately, the choice to be in a marriage of mixed religion comes down to how you can respect each other's choices. If that is possible, most likely the relationship can flourish. Before entering in a marriage, it is best to discuss the important aspects of each of your religious beliefs. After all, while religion makes up an important part of many marriages, great communication and mutual respect make up a huge part of it too.

In Christendom the language is clear. Christian marriage is founded on the instruction in Genesis that "a man leaves his parents, cleave, and be united with his wife." However, in a changing age when living together before marriage appears to be the norm, and divorce is growing ever more common, some Christian attitudes toward marriage, sex, and the family may be changing. This section will seek to look at different Christian attitudes toward sex and relationships, including the role of contraception and the purposes of marriage. Love is the doctrine, to which one submits and obeys to have a marriage that lasts until death. Morality is highly advocated in this religion and disobedience brings its own curse and makes life a living hell.

Islam also advocates morality in marriages for couples who love deeply. I believe so many other religions also share the same view about "love and unity" of couples in marriages and their families. Sexual behavior in many societies is determined by codes of morality - cultural taboos, religious injunctions, and unscientific conclusions (e.g. HIV/AIDS). On matters related to human sexuality, the western world tends to be polarized between social and religious conservatives and liberals and this is where matters of relationships and marriages become big problems. Topics on human sexuality form a large part of the moral code for most Christian denominations and individuals, and to the really "the born-again" Muslims. For many, sex in marital relationships form the most important segment of morality. Morals and values are important and must be formed in any society that wants to live in peace and harmony. Adolescent sexuality frequently catches the interest of researchers, policy makers, and health practitioners who at the end of their researches, policies and health observations, have no solution to curb the problems.

Hardy & Raffaelli emphasized that degeneration of values is often the source of the trend toward earlier sexual behavior (Elliott, 2005). My personal observation from traveling around West African countries, scouting news for Life Herald Publications, shows that children with a strong religious background are less likely to have sex earlier than children with a less religious background. Perhaps their religious views lead to view the consequences of having sex early or illicitly as negative. Adults also view divorce and having children outside marriage as negative and evil. Religious beliefs reduce the likelihood of adolescents engaging in early sex by shaping their attitudes and beliefs about sexual activity. Religious beliefs shape adult attitudes toward divorce and extra-marital affairs as shameful for the family.

There are religious bodies whose belief systems contain prohibitions. These beliefs are the spiritual life of the practitioners who hold the beliefs in high regard. Considering the honor and dignity they uphold in their religion, it would be a devastating evil and disgrace for these religious practitioners and their families to associate with immorality, involving sicknesses like HIV/AIDS, STDS, pregnancies outside wedlock, and abortions.

Commandments are laws that raise the moral standards of a society and are not evil. Liberty is a good thing but without limits it is destructive. To love our children is great and humane, but loving them without accountability is the worst crime parents and society can commit against children. Where there are no laws, no prohibitions, no religious beliefs, and no moral standards, the breakdown of social order assured. This is exactly what is happening in our society today.

According to **Pearce and Haynie**, the relationship between religion and crime has a long history. Parental attendance of religious services and their strong belief in God appears to protect against serious delinquency (Elliott, 2005).

Governments and societies across the globe are trying greatly to control juvenile delinquency but on a wrong axis they place their might policing, more efficient courts, and improved correctional programs, and too little emphasis on community programs that give families the support they need to deal with delinquency. Delinquencies of today grow into tomorrow's state crimes. Religious beliefs shape behaviors and discourage criminal behaviors and intentions. People brought up in religious homes are the great and successful leaders and models of any society. Although, there are various reasons why people divorce, but the most outstanding is that there is no prohibition and moral instruction in the home. Religion at any rate is a great reformer.

We, as people, have wandered too far from the truth. Our societies have been attacked and overrun by philosophy and psychology based on human knowledge. Society exposes religion as a part of pop life and culture. Religious themes should be incorporated into Hollywood, Nollywood, Bollywood, and many other woods, to make faith, religion and spirituality more prominent in our televisions shows. When more sacredness and truth are viewed, then there will be many more changes in family settings and homes.

When we encourage more religious movies, songs, and stories in our homes and family gatherings, and talk more about them in our cultural settings, our society will become better. Programs and films that have religious content might give teenagers and adults something to think about regarding behaviors to encourage and avoid. Let religious leaders be friendly and live peaceful and harmonious lives with others and never discriminate against others. They must know that God is Almighty and All-knowing and none of them can influence God or fight for God. God is greater than all and can destroy those who hate Him within a twinkle of an eye. God desires that we worship in TRUTH and demonstrate LOVE for one another.

Chapter 5
How Destructive Divorce is to a Nation

Civilization has done much to improve the life of individuals on earth: look at the communication system, look at transportation system, health system and many other systems that address human needs. Man has acquired so much knowledge, that children are now born into a world where men no longer have time to sit and ponder about life. Thank God for the educated advocates who are there for us in every field, who will coach and guide us to success in our problems. Parents are out on the street seeking wealth and have no time to raise their children. To handle a relationship, one needs an adequate knowledge; marriage relationship for example is more than just living together and sex. If you have no idea of religious principles, and have no beliefs and teachings to rest on, your only option is to seek the services of a good relationship-and-marriage counselor. Relationships are very expensive. A little mistake can ruin your marriage and tear your world apart for life. Our greatest anchor must be God. You need to depend on God, your spiritual leaders, your parents (if they are there for you), and a good relationship counselor. You need someone to guide you and be an encouragement in your relationship. Whatever your situation, you should always pray for direction because the only one who knows every heart and situation is God.

A marriage united in love and peace is a pillar of society, no matter how carelessly we consider it. It is also the pillar of government, business, and the military. Marriage cuts to the very heart of a nation. As goes marriage; so goes the nation. It infiltrates every aspect of human life- not only for the married, but also for the unmarried. When marriages prosper, the nation rises; when marriages fail, the nation falls. Divorce not only rattles the foundation of the judicial system and psychiatry, but, through its influence on children, alters the course of the next generation. Divorces are the steps to the grave of a culture and a nation. The study of culture, social or family, is the study of marriage. Where there is neither religion, culture, nor spiritual beliefs, nor knowledge of God, society wanders aimlessly in neighborhoods of broken homes and broken lives.

How Destructive Divorce Is

Divorce is destroying our society in all sectors, ripping away the foundation of families and tearing apart the lives of children who will be the leaders of tomorrow. Our society has lost its basic fundamental strength of the family unit. Children who grow up in homes of divorce are less likely to succeed in life; they do poorly in school, do develop bad habits, and have unresolved issues of abandonment and feelings of rejection. Children feel hopeless for their parents' divorce. They think the society hates them and are insecure, and their parents hate them more. They hate life Children raised with single parents do not do as well as children raised in a nuclear family with both the biological mother and father. Children who are raised with step-parents are at a higher risk of abuse and neglect, feeling unloved and unwanted than children raised in families with both parents, even when those parents have problems.

Studies have shown that children of divorced or single parents do much worse in school, do not learn self-esteem, or develop self-confidence. Our children are the ones who pay the ultimate price for divorced parents.

When our children are harmed during childhood as a result of divorce or broken homes, they are less successful adults compared to children who were lovingly brought up by parents. Our society depends on healthy and developed children to grow up and take on the roles of the current adults. When we don't ensure the health and safety of our children, we are ruining our society and placing it in harms den.

Society depends on the healthy structure of the family unit. When that unit becomes fractured and splintered, the children become fractured and splintered as well. Children turn to the streets for the love and acceptance they are not receiving at home. When children turn to the streets, they are ensured of not receiving the developmental needs of healthy growth and maturity. Their view of the world is altered, and they see it as a cruel place in which survival depends on who is the strongest. This world view harms society by making it less civilized.

Children whose home lives are splintered are injured in major ways. They miss out on healthy, structured, and loving environments and come to view marriage as expendable or of no real worth or value. Today we have a high divorce rate as a result. Divorce and adults choosing to "live together" rather than "get married" are responsible for many of the ills our society faces today. When children are raised by parents who do not make a fully committed relationship, when the parents refuse to marry, this leaves children feeling unimportant, hopeless, and in a volatile situation in which security is not available. Children know when their parents are not truly committed to each other, and they internalize this knowledge as something lacking within them. Children are unable to believe their parents are capable of wrong doing. They get their world view from their parents. If parents refuse to fully commit to one another, the children feel the parents are not committed to them either.

Children of divorced homes often come together and live in

their own world of abandonment and hopelessness. For the sake of safety and living sense of belonging, they form gangs to regard as their own family.

Our families are our most vital asset in society. When our families are splintered or if we refuse to truly form a secured and committed family unit, our children suffer greatly. When I look around and see splintered families, children who are lost on the street, and at the shelters, I see our society as torn apart.

If children do not receive a solid foundation with stability, structure, proper discipline, and education of what a family is, and how one functions, our society fails. We fall into a society of selfish individuals who always place their own needs above those of anyone else. A selfish society becomes incapable of meeting its needs. Focused solely on our own needs, society cannot function well.

Society was formed from two important needs of mankind. First is the need for companionship to avoid isolation. Babies who do not receive adequate touch, fail to thrive and will die. That is how important human companionship and relationships are. The second need is for safety and survival. We are unable to survive alone; we need numbers to provide protection and safety. This is why humans have banded together into groups and made rules for all to follow. Without rules, a society fails.

Divorce is very bad for society and I want all the divorce advocates to know that. I do not believe anyone should live with abuse. I think our society has removed all the natural factors that maintain relationships. We jump into relationships and marriages too soon and without understanding. Our youth do not have the capabilities of commitment to anybody. They think marriage and love relationships lack importance and are disposable. They will not even marry the mother or father of their children, not only is this extremely sad, but the consequences are dire to the survival and health of society. I strongly believe our society is extremely harmed by the splintering of our family units, culture and faith. Now that these units are splintered and not being reformed, we are in a critical stage of societal breakdown. I hope people will realize just how important the marriage and family unit is and take some affirmative action to reactivate strength and stability back into our family units.

If we cannot hold onto cultural and religious beliefs and live like humans instead of little gods or animals, then, the marriage union will not be preserved. Marriage should require extensive education of what is means to be married and how to handle problems that may occur within a marriage. I also think that divorce should be made more difficult to obtain. The law should require extensive counseling to couples before granting a divorce. I also think we should encourage parents to make a great commitment to relationships that already involve children. Government and society should give benefit and encouragement to married couples and united families and totally discourage giving benefits to so-called single partners. If we do this, then people will need to marry in order to receive marriage benefits. Why should a society reward people who do not make a marriage commitment for the sake of their children anyway? The "easy come and easy go" in marriage is only making it easier for our society to become ever more fractured at the family unit level. Marriage should be a commitment and a vow to the society and to the children who would be blessed by the union.

I firmly believe that our families are our greatest asset and strength as a society. We need to do all we can to bring them back to life and stabilize them. Again, the society should recognize and reward those who do make that real commitment.

There is need for our society to gain strength and health, and enough to seeing our families falling apart, it is our children who suffer the most for it. What does it teach children when their parents refuse to marry or choose just flirt around in a society? What type of example does that set for our children? Why it is so difficult for people to understand that marriage is not just a religious matter but also a matter of the health and stability of society? On the other hand, no matter what religion you are in, it is right to dedicate your marriage to God because God is the only power every individual can rely on. God does not suffer from your failure if you don't rely on Him; it is you and the society who suffer it. It is as simple as that. We should not stake our unity and future happiness of our children on the liberty and freedom to make bad choices.

How to Find a Good Marriage Counselor?

By their fruits we shall know them. A good marriage counselor can be known by the work he or she does within his or her community. Good works can't be hidden; people in that community must commend or testify about that counselor. We can know a good marriage counselor by his or her own marital status. Does he or she have a successful marriage? Is he or she living in love and harmony with his or her spouse? We can also consider his or her family relationship. Who are his or her children? What do his or her children do? What social life and friends do they choose? Do they live on the streets or in the shelters? Nobody can argue with proof. How many marriages have he or she restored, how many relationships has he or she revived? These questions will definitely help an individual to choose a marriage counselor for the success of marriage relationship. If you don't understand it, don't handle it. Relationships are very fragile. When marriage is destroyed, the couple will suffer, the society will suffer, and the children will suffer most. Choose a counselor, through prayer, tell him or her the truth, confide in him or her and by the grace of God, you will be blessed with a stronger marriage.

CAUSES AND EFFECTS OF DIVORCE AND BROKEN HOMES IN OUR SOCIETY

Chapter 6
Personal Information and Pretense

There are many factors that contribute to the problem of divorce and broken homes in our society and these factors vary in different societies and cultures. Faithless lifestyle, education, and civilization are among these contributing factors. Many countries of the world have over-stretched liberty, to the point of anarchy. No man or government is wiser than God. God gave the Ten Commandments as guideline for His people to live by. There should be commandments in our homes and in our societies. Ignorance is a chronic disease. Many civilized nations are ignorant about the power of culture in marriage, ignorant about unity in family, ignorant about religious beliefs. Ignorance is not excusable. What we do not understand costs us our peace and happiness. This is what we are experiencing in our society today.

Personal Information

Information is a powerful tool in every aspect of human endeavor, especially the information about yourself. It affects human relationships and advancement. Without information, relationships as well as development become static and fail to advance. Information can build or destroy; the use of it is what determines its effects. A piece of information can destroy an entirely good reputation, as well as salvage an individual from wreckage. Information is vital in human relationships, friendships, love relationships, and in marriage relationships.

Everyone works with information that determines one's character. Miss-used or faulty information can cause a total collapse in relationships. All relationships should begin with openness, honesty, and trust. So many people begin a relationship with lies. They lie about their family, about their financial and educational background, and their past or present love life. Playing with information always ends up breaking hearts and trust. A true relationship is based on" love me as I am."

Evil Outcomes of False Personal Information in Relationships

Husbands and wives, boyfriends and girlfriends, lie to each other a lot. Our romantic relationships are seldom what they seem because of lies and deceits in the start of the relationship. We all want a relationship that is built on openness, intimacy, and trust, yet lovers often lie about their true feelings for each other, the reason they fell in love, and lie about their level of commitment.

Our romantic relationships are full of paradoxes. Every day, couples or lovers struggle to cover their initial lies with more lies and secrecy until the entire relationship is based on nothing but suspicions, secrets, and fear. Once you allow a lie in relationship, you live in worry. You don't want to be caught, especially when the relationship seems good enough to keep.

We all should know that truth sets every individual free. How can you prepare yourself to face your partner when you are not exactly what you appear or claim `to be? The shame can even cause some people their health and confidence for life. A relationship is like a public servant who chooses to be faithful to all the people he or she serves. One cannot be sure if the people one serves – among could be one's employer or boss.

Women lie a lot when they start a new relationship. Some women claim to be virgins, some claim to be very sophisticated and educated. Women talk about their family with great honor, like being from a very rich or royal family. Some women live with a husband or boyfriend and tell another she lives with her uncle or brother. Some have a sugar daddy who they tell their new boyfriend is father; and some women do not ever show their home to their boyfriends because they said they live in ultra-modern homes while they really live in project houses.

Now read this true story. In 2011, a young lady went shopping and met a handsome young man who saw her and approached her. The young man really loved her at first sight and paid for the things she picked. During their conversation, the lady told him she was a student, raised in a Christian home. Her mother is a very strict woman and does not encourage relationships outside marriage. Because of her mother's standards, she has never loved and she is a virgin. This young man was so happy that he had found a life partner and started doing things for her. He did not know that it was all fake false information. As time went by, the young lady discovered that the young man was serious about the relationship, and had been truthful about himself from the very first day. The situation became a worry to the lady. The young man was really in charge and very humble. The young lady fell in love but very confused about all the fake information she had given the man about herself, especially that she was a virgin. As the relationship grew stronger, the lady knew it was time to know each other. One day she went to the store and bought glue, because she wanted to protect her relationship but did not know how to undo the fake information. She bought the glue and applied it into her vagina to restore her virginity, at least for their first night. The result was terrible. After about six hours, the lady could not urinate, and her health was affected. She fainted and was taken to the hospital where hospital staff discovered glue in her vagina. Doctors operated her and she survived. The young man was shocked and eventually backed out of the relationship. The lady was devastated. She lost the best man she had ever met in her entire life. She survived the surgery, but she did not save the relationship. The relationship did not survive because of the false information she gave about herself. She experienced shame at the hospital and the news about her was posted on Facebook.

All these embarrassments resulted from the faulty information she gave about her status. There is profit in telling the truth. If someone cannot love you for whom and what you are, it is better you both stay unconnected.

A couple divorced just last year because of false information his wife gave him about herself when they first met. The wife told him that she lost her parents when she was very young and there was nobody to support her when she wanted to go to college. She also told her husband that she never married in her life and had no children. The husband loved her and they got married. One day she told her husband that she wanted to travel to another state to visit her friend who helped her when she was in that state. The husband accepted and let her go. She never told the man that she was once married and had two grown-up daughters. This woman changed her names but the reason she did that was known only to her. Two months later, her husband was at home alone when a call came in and he answered. The caller asked to speak to Shirley, (the wife's real name) and identified herself as Shirley's daughter. The man told her she had the wrong number. As the conversation went further, this girl confirmed to the man that her mother had been with them two months ago and had called the State too. This man was embarrassed. As devil might have arranged it, Shirley's cell phone was switched off and she did not know. She had given her daughters the house phone number and told them to ask for Joan whenever they called. She did not tell them details about the false information she had given her new husband. There is nothing that can remain secret forever.

Her husband discovered all the lies his wife had told about herself and their relationship began to soar. Gradually this couple no longer trusted each other. The husband was disappointed because he did not marry who she claimed to be and thought of himself as a fool. He filed for a divorce.

Tell the truth about yourself. It does not matter how ugly your past is. Let your partner or loved ones know you are a new person believing God to be the best person. If he or she truly loves you, he or she will value the relationship. Do not entangle yourself because you want to prove that you are an angel. Do not say you are white when you are brown. The immediate pride always ends up in shame. Endure the shame in the beginning to establish your future happiness.

Men give false information to boost their ego. Young men who have no job lie that they are in universities. They say that they are sons of rich men, and sons of men in government. Some men survive through sugar mommies who they represent as their mothers. Men rent luxury trucks to boost their morale and impress ladies that they are wealthy.

Relationships should be based on who you are being good and happy with a life partner who is content with being who he or she is. It is even better to hide all your riches and let a relationship be formed because of true love. Apart from being discovered as fake person, you may add stress to your life trying to be what you are not. If you fall in love for material things like wealth, fame, and power, know that these material things can fade, and once they start fading, the relationship may also start to fade. It is only love that remains and never fades. Base any relationship on love and avoid lies in any form.

PRETENSE

This is the act of faking your real self, your real character, your real knowledge, your real standard in education, finance, society and current issues of life. Some people have given so much fake information about themselves that they constantly struggle to uphold what they have said about themselves. This is very stressful, tiresome, and horrible. I understand that some people can fake being sick for a little while, but no sick person can fake being well for a long time. This is the case of individuals who try to act as the personality they pretend to be. Some people pretend that they are from wealthy homes and spend all their time in a relationship talking big and borrowing money to live big. Some of these people even rent big cars to visit their intended friend or lover. Some go about claiming to be students of different universities when they never finished secondary school. Some even claim to be sons and daughters of government leaders. An acquaintance who has been divorced for three years now told me what he did to marry the daughter of a rich business man.

"The first step I took was to make up a story. I listed all the elements I wanted the story to have and practiced until I learned each and every aspect by heart. If I make up things as I go or at the instant, I might end up contradicting myself or forgetting the vital parts. Another step: I got some designer items like brand name outfits and accessories. Went for a complete reshuffle of the collection in my wardrobe. To pretend to be one of the members of the higher class, I needed to learn certain basic expressions and be aware of the vocabulary used by the rich people. Know about the cuisine, fashion, and current events that the rich people prefer. This I also perfected.

Do not flaunt your so-called wealth or expensive items. Rich people automatically know the classy items from the cheap ones. Never, ever go for fakes. They are likely to be identified very easily. I had very few but original. Etiquette is very important for rich people. Display a good code of conduct. Learn the proper way to speak, sit, eat, and walk, and so on. Also, address others using properly spelled titles.

If you are dining with friends, make sure to pay a handsome tip to the waiter. Do not pay what a middle-class man would. Remember, you are pretending to be from a well-to-do family. Each time I took her out; I did spend a lot and tipped the waiters well.

Support a charity or a trust. At the same time, make sure you are seen and known by everyone present there, for your good manners and nature. I did give some used things to a shelter with pictures.

All these I did and eventually we fell in love and got married, I thought that once we married, it would not matter anymore and I would try to handle it, but it was not easy and she discovered all. Right then we started disagreeing and things went out of control. She filed for divorce and that was it"

Don't pretend to be who you are not. Start from scratch, work hard and trust God for increase. You will be where you aim someday. If you aim for stars but miss your target somewhere along the line, you will still be in heavenly territory.

Chapter 7
LIES IN THE FORMATION PERIOD IN A RELATIONSHIP

Lies are harmful to all relationships, but are especially, poisonous to love and marriage relationships. My dad used to tell me and my siblings when we were kids. "Mr. Lie is a man with short legs, he neither runs too fast nor too slow. There is a man whose legs are long but he never sets off in time. Whenever he does, Mr. Truth always catches and overtakes Mr. Lie." There are basic things a man needs to know in life before doing anything: What is this that I am about to do? What do I want to achieve? What is my integrity in this whole matter? What will be the final result? They are simple questions but their responses offer protection for the future. Anything you build on a fake foundation, it has just too short of a life span. There is no magic except truth to cure this. The most intimate relationship in life is marriage. It entails a lot and there is no shame, no secret that love or marriage will not reveal. Let there be nothing that will make you desperate or cause you to be consciously alert all the time. Let there be no walls, or anything that you would never want to discuss. All these raise curiosity, and the end result is discovery.

There could be mistake, it is far better than lies, because the man doesn't exist who has never made a mistake. It is only God who cannot make a mistake. He is all-knowing God. Satan makes mistake all the time. Mistakes can be explained and forgiven; but a lie might not be forgiven because it is done on purpose and it is willful. Lies and mistakes both have the power to destroy relationships.

LIES THAT LOVERS AND COUPLES TELL ONE ANOTHER

It is not fun to think about the terrible lies people tell to their spouses. But, at the same time, people tend to be curious about the topics which couples try to hide and conceal from each other. This is a scene where "the pot calls kettle black". The husband has something he is hiding from the wife and yet curious to know what the wife is hiding. The wife has made up her mind that the husband is not truthful and is hiding something and would what to know what it is. Both of them are guilty of lying and hiding issues yet accuses each other of being a liar.

In 1979 during a vacation from elementary school, three of my maternal cousins from different cities and I were on holidays to visit our grandma. One afternoon while we were playing football behind the house, Grandma came back from the market and called us to come to the house. We all went and greeted her with, "Welcome, Granny." She said, " How are you all, my children?" We answered, "Fine Granny." After a few minutes, Grandma took out a pack of cookies and placed it on the table. She looked at us and asked. "Who opened the kitchen door?" We all looked at each other suspiciously and turned to Grandma, but Tony looked at Grandma and said,' Granny! I did not eat meat. Look at my hand; nothing on it, mama. Grandma burst into laughter and said, "Tony I did not ask who ate meat. I asked who opened the kitchen door. "Grandma shared the cookies among the three of us who did not say anything but gave Tony a good beating. This example shows how couples jump the gun and fight to cover their lies and protect their shame. Living in a curious situation every day is hell in a relationship. In my years of counseling, I found that partners hide many things from each other, which they introduced to gain certain credits or pride in the beginning of their relationship. Here are some of the common lies partners tell to each other daily.

Too busy to see each other often: one or the other or both live separately and lie about being too busy to spend time with the other. This is a result of other relationships he or she keeps and would not want partner to know about it. So they lie to each other about busy schedules, career pursuits, and family laws.

Lovers lie to each other about their past life and relationships: Past lives and relationships is a big one. Partners always want to appear as angels to each other. They think that if a partner knows about their past love life, it might destroy trust and respect. A friend once told me that knowing a woman's past is ugly thing to do because every woman has a bit of bad past. But men are expected to have bad past and all societies accept it.

Ex-boyfriends and girlfriends: Lovers lie about feelings they have; loving the present partner more than the ex-partner or not having any feelings at all about the ex when they do. They reassure each other of their commitment and the feeling they have for each other but in actuality, they still have secrets/feelings they hide.

Health issues: During the time I was counseling, I discovered that lovers knew nothing about health situation of their partner. A partner had seizures but was hiding it, until the day she suffered one in the presence of her boyfriend, she was ashamed. She told the boyfriend she just experienced it for the first time.

Financial security: Lovers hide their true financial status. They lie to each other about how much they are financially secured and pretend to be at ease financially.

Betraying confidence: Normally, relationship issues/problems are supposed to be between partners, but some partners discuss their love life, and/or problems with friends and loved ones instead of with each other.

MISTAKES

A mistake is anything that one does with the intention of producing a good result but ends up producing a bad result in words or deeds. Mistakes are very detrimental to marriage or love relationships but can be corrected through dialogue and explanation. It sometimes leaves a scar of reference on the person.

People think that mistakes are merely little things that can be over looked, but in many cases, the " little things" add up and cause the end of marriages or relationships. Let us look at some of these mistakes closely.

Holding Secrets

This is dangerous in a relationship because when a secret is discovered, it could be interpreted in a different light. No matter how bad an issue is, it must be shared. It is better to forgo becoming involved in a relationship than to be disgraced in ending a relationship, Let everything be brought to light; and that will save your face.

Everyone has a few secrets but, let them be made know because you are in a serious relationship. Keeping secrets because they are embarrassing, harmful, or fearful of a partner's action or possible rejection for a relationship is like hiding a tattle snake in a room. Bring it up before it shows up on its own.

Keeping secrets is harmful in marriages or love relationships. Keeping secrets often prevents people from dealing with the problem at hand. Keeping secrets leads to increased stress, anxiety, and it often makes people think about the issue emotionally. This can cause frequent mistakes.

People who have a secret crush on someone often dwell on their feelings more than people who are able to talk about such things out in the open. Keeping secrets can make things seem more important than they really are. Likewise, revealing secrets is very helpful when it is done right; that is, in a safe, non-judgmental environment.

Revealing secrets can reduce stress by helping people let go of an issue and think more clearly. If a secret is bothering you, it really does help to get it off your chest.

Sharing a secret with your lover or your spouse makes you free all the time and allows you to be a better partner.

SOME MISTAKES SPOUSES DO

Building Walls against a Partner

Some people build walls around their partner to prevent them from relating with others. A friend I used to know called it being protective and would not allow his partner to see people, make friends, or even interact with neighbors, Each time I asked him why he felt the need to be so protective of her, he would say that he did not want anybody to corrupt her and inspire her against him. But this raised her curiosity as to why this man should fear people. "Is there anything my husband is hiding form me?" The search to know what it is begins here. This is a terrible mistake in relationship.

Nagging Is Not a Discussion

When you have nothing to say to your partner, teach him or her to sing, teach him or her something that gives both of you the chance to laugh and be happy rather than to criticize, condemn and gossip. Do not ever want to seek fault; just find a way to offer praises - this will help build a strong foundation.

Do Not Betray Your Spouse

Betrayal comes in many forms. Whether it is in the form of cheating, or even something as insignificant as sharing his or her problem with a member of his or her family, sharing private information with people other than your partner is bad. Betrayal is a real killer of relationships, and one that is difficult to be forgiven of and to forgive. As they say, once trust is lost, it is extremely difficult to regain. He who betrays his spouse has already betrayed himself.

Do Not Check Up On Your Partner Excessively

There is a thin line between caring about your partner's well-being and being overly protective of him or her. However, if you find the need to follow your partner's every move and question their whereabouts and motives constantly, then perhaps you need to learn to give your partner space. Part of trust lies in allowing one another to lead lives without scrutiny.

Insensitivity and Being Unsupportive to a Partner is Bad

Supporting your partner's needs, goals, and decisions is imperative in your relationship. The one person that we always want to be able to count on for emotional support is our significant other. With that being said, when you belittle the ideas and goals of your partner (or ignore them altogether), your partner feels misunderstood, unimportant in your eyes, or even rejected. Bring the two of you closer together by being a pillar of support.

Do Not Fight to Be "Right" in Argument

Whether you realize it or not, most arguments are about the same thing. What I mean is, when you argue with someone, what you are generally doing is trying to prove to the other person that you are "right" or that they should share your opinion. However, doing this is a dead-end approach to anything. Instead, you need to let go of the prize of being "right" in order to avoid arguing excessively and without ever reaching a resolution to the real problem in your relationship.

Do Not Let the Relationship Become Stale

Let's be frank. When your relationship started, there were dates that you constantly went on. You bought each other random gifts and did things for one another spontaneously out of kindness. But, as time went on and the two of you became more comfortable with one another, all of those spontaneous bits and pieces that created the sparks and excitement in your relationship diminished completely. It is important that you never let your relationship become boring and stale. Keep dating. Spend time together often; doing the things you both love to do.

Everything you do, to create fun in your relationship has its impact on the future life of you and your partner's relationship. Put in some positive effort, and reap the rewards. Make one or more of the preceding mistakes, however, and watch as your partner drifts further and further away until there is nothing left of the love relationship.

Mistakes are little things that destroy much. Just know some of them, avoid them, and save your relationship. There is no perfect relationship out there waiting for you but make the one you have perfect.

Do Not Do These Provocatively

Do not interrogate your partner. Do not be suspicious, or ask someone about your partner's privacy or what he or she does when at work. Do not hack into your partner's emails or listen to phone calls secretly. Do not trail your partner or have an affair with his or her friends. Do not isolate, do not gossip about his or her relatives and do not search out information about his or her past sex life.

Cheating in a Relationship

Both male and female cheat. This is rather unfortunate, they do not understand marriage relationship is a vow to God and it must be kept sacred. Infidelity (unfaithfulness) or extramarital affairs have been extensively studied over the past two decades. When it comes to infidelity, two related explanations have been given. The first explanation is probably the most well-known: Spouses cheat because of problems in their relationship. Something is missing in sex, pursuing a career, travels, passion has faded, or partners feel lonely. People find someone who treats them better or who appreciates them more than their current spouse, and so on. Some partners claim that they are not happy in their relationship so they look for love and affection elsewhere. Both excuses are correct at surface view but it is wrong to cheat. Even though it is our nature, it is more rewarding to control our sexual urge for people that are not our partners.

Why is being faithful to one's spouse so difficult for many people to do? This is where conscience comes in. Is this right? If I discover that my spouse is cheating on me, how will I feel, can I handle this? Do to others what you would want them to do to you. Cheating in a relationship is a cancer that may be terminal.

Chapter 8
ASSUMPTION AND EXPECTATION FACTOR

In a relationship, many people always assume that their partner knows what is right and will act accordingly. This is wrong because of knowledge and character differences. In a relationship, teaching and learning never end. One must, at all times, be ready to teach his or her partner what he or she knows without grumbling or irritation, as well to learn from one's partner without shame or anger. This kind of foundation in a relationship creates an atmosphere of understanding friendliness.

Assumptions in Relationships

Reasonable individuals are slow to make assumptions. They check the facts, ask questions, and explore other perspectives before moving forward in their thinking or behavior. By contrast, those who live in dysfunctional mental health routinely make faulty and even dangerous assumptions.

WHY PEOPLE MAKE ASSUMPTIONS

People make assumption for many reasons in a relationship. If these assumptions are not done in an atmosphere of love and peace the end of it is negative to marriage relationships. Below are some of the reasons couples or lovers make assumptions.

During breakdown in communication

When there is no communication between couples or partners due to disagreements, quarrels, arguments, or fights, communication breaks down. Couples or partners who are not communicating can assume what or where the partner could be up to. What is he or she thinking about and perhaps what he or she is about to do next. This is bad in a relationship.

To avoid confrontation

When there is no good relationship between couples or lovers, they do everything possible to avoid open confrontation. This situation always keep couples far apart, but because they are still in relationship, probably live in the same house, assumption is the only world they can share with for each other.

To avoid / ease tension

Many people assume in their relationship because they don't want to escalate tension. They do as much as possible to avoid each other's presence, avoid talking to one another, not to say anything that might explode their grievances.

To reduce fear

Assumptions reduce fear in a relationship. For example if there is a problem between couples who have lived together for a long time, one will assume that he or she has known his or her partner for so long and can't go to the extend to do something horrible, and assume that his or her partner cannot do that because he or she never did such a thing before., Assumption reduces fear of been taken on unaware.

To test partner's intelligence

People make assumptions in a relationship because they want to test how intelligent or clever their partners are. Other people do it because they want to know how closely both couples are in thoughts and actions. They want to know how living together for long time has created similarity in their behavior.

To find fault in another

People make assumptions because they want to find faults with other. Finding fault gives them a chance for confrontation. This type of assumption is done in a relationship that is sick and close to dissolving.

Assumptions are generally dangerous. Many people have been reduced to nothing because of assumption; many sweet relationships have fallen apart because of making assumptions. Families and friends have separated and remain enemies, while many people made some bad financial investment because of an assumption. Great numbers of people are depressed and frustrated because of assumption. Assumption may give you a short-term peace or excitement, but it also creates dangerous pain and destruction thereafter. Do not assume. Find out the facts and live by the true knowledge of what is right.

Outcome of assumptions in most cases, are ugly

Look at the relationships in your life. How many times have you made assumptions about what people will like or dislike? How will people react to issues or something you need to tell them, or even things they think in their minds? What motivates them? What are their desires in life?

When we know someone and we have been in a long-term relationship, such as husband and wife, parent and children or the people we work with every day, we believe we know them, what they think and how they react to things. No, it is very hard to know what is in one's mind at a particular moment.

When we work on developing a relationship in any way, whether it is rebuilding a broken relationship or striving to strengthen an existing one, or developing a brand new relationship, we make assumptions. We are very likely not to be successful in our endeavors when we build our relationships on a foundation of assumptions. The relationships will at some point, falter and begin to suffer because some of the assumptions we made, will not be correct.

If we have built a great foundation for our relationship, no assumptions were made, the foundation is rock solid. Over the years we begin to assume that we know our partners so well that we know exactly how they feel, think and react. One might think it is safe to make assumptions in this case; however, what we often overlook is that people change. We change all the time. What we liked and the way we reacted a year ago may be quite different from the way we think and react today. As individuals, we grow and change. If the other person does not recognize the changes and assumes that everything is always the same, then the assumptions they make can often begin to unravel the relationship.

In a nut shell, weather you are new in a relationship or you are in a hundred-year-old relationship, it is not safe to make assumptions about the other persons' feelings, thoughts, reactions and actions.

How to remove assumptions in a relationship

The first step is to become aware of what we are assuming. Many of our assumptions are so ingrained that we may not even recognize we are making an assumption. We must work with facts to be sure of what we do in our relationship. Assumptions can be critical to the health of a relationship.

Once we realize that we have not interacted with the other person about the issue, then it is an assumption. You need to ask questions right there. The simplest way to dump our assumptions is to ask questions. Make sure you project the questions correctly across to your partner as caring and loving. Your questions will be received as having a sincere interest in the other person and this will strengthen and, in some cases, revitalize your relationship.

Don't ever assume. Find out the facts. That will make you a better partner and secure your relationship.

EXPECTATIONS

Expectation is an unspoken word or thought that the mind concludes to be true. It is a dangerous mind game that has killed and damaged many souls. On real-life issues, I do tell my friends to build their expectation on God who never fails and never disappoints rather than putting it on man. Man changes, man dies, man fails, and man forgets, so these attributes of man never favor expectation.

We humans create expectations for ourselves and for our family members and close associates consciously or unconsciously. Expectation is a human trait of projecting one's own desires and thoughts onto the people with whom they are closest. We tend to expect significant people in our lives to behave in a manner envisioned in our mind. Expectations in relationships can be harmful when unspoken ideals are projected onto the other person. Assumptions and unrealistic expectations collectively sabotage or destroy relationships.

Many people have their feelings hurt because they mistakenly expected that someone else knew what they wanted. Have you ever become annoyed or angry with someone who acted differently than you expected? Have you found yourself saying, "If you really loved me, you would … or "Why did you not…?" and "You should have…."

It does not really matter what kind of relationship you are in. Each person's expectations play a large role in determining the health of any relationship. Perceptions of a relationship change when there is a contrast between the ideal and the real. The partnership commitments strengthen when each partner begins to see the relationship for what it really is.

Having unfulfilled expectations is a sure way to ruin a relationship. When an individual has a strong desire for their partner to meet impossible expectations, they become nonchalant and blinded to whom their partner really is. Even if the partner tries to meet the expectations, it will never be exactly what their partner wants. This is because expectations in relationships are most often unattainable. We all have a preconceived notion of what we want in our ideal mate, and this is how expectations are conceived.

Expectations in marriage relationship

A person experiences different types of expectations in his or her life: parent/child, friendship, romantic, and business. Different types of expectations do negatively affect our relationships. Expectations can be unrealistic, unclear, unnamed, unfulfilled, unspoken, unexpressed, misunderstood, and misguided. These unrealistic expectations can come from our family values and traditions, past relationships, and past experiences.

Individual's past affect expectations in a relationship

Experiences we had in life shape how we think, feel, and act. Various influences in life can cause us to form unclear and even unrealistic expectations. Key influences that shape our beliefs include childhood upbringing, gender, age, cultural differences, traumatic events, and religious and political beliefs. Each person is a compilation and product of their past history. Along the way, we each learn by trial and error how to get our needs met and one desires fulfilled.

The quality of interactions with significant others from birth onward have an effect on the way we view the world. Our childhood upbringing influences who we become and plays a role in the formation of personal expectations. We learn through experimentation. We learn whether we can trust ourselves and others. We learn to feel worthy and confident, or ashamed and guilty of whom we are. This is imprinted at an early age and is unconsciously set into motion. These lessons form the core of our belief system. This is where misguided relationship expectations can begin.

Each person brings into a relationship their own family values. While growing up, you internalize your own family's beliefs. When a person grows up in a family where their parents don't take the time or interest to listen to them, this can lead to the child growing up feeling no one cares what they think. The domino effect of this is that the individual does not verbalize what they need or feel; yet still feels disappointed when their partner does not automatically figure out how they are feeling. For example, if in your upbringing it was emphatic that you were never to bother your father or mother when they were busy, you learn to push your feelings down and keep them suppressed. As a consequence, entering a romantic relationship makes you feel unworthy of expressing your needs and feelings. Unfortunately, this can lead to resentment and anger because the other person does not automatically know how you are feeling and cannot possibly know how to help you.

Most of us are not aware of our unspoken rules and expectations, until the other person violates them. When our partner does not live up to our unrealistic expectations, we may become frustrated, disappointed or angry. Often we don't even know why we are upset because we don't know what is wrong. It is helpful to reflect on "'the rules" of one's family so that misguided assumptions and expectations are brought out for examination.

How expectations can affect marriage

Misguided expectations pose the biggest danger when each person in a relationship brings their own, and sometimes conflicting, expectations to the relationship. The couple would be prone to consistent disagreement and contentions.

As we project our viewpoint onto others, we believe that they think and feel in a similar way that we would in the same situation, and we expect them to behave accordingly. Unspoken expectation is unrealistic and dangerous in relationships. When a spouse projects onto their partner what they want or need without knowledge or agreement about it. This affects their love and friendship in their relationship. Your partner cannot read your mind; you have to discuss every idea or thought together to agree. When a partner does something that seems in deep contrast with the standards they have associated with each other, he or she often feels hurt, betrayed, angry and /or confused and love and happiness in the relationship fall. Disappointment gets expressed in the kinds of phrases we have heard or spoken: "You are the last person I ever expected to do that," "you really let me down, and this is not like you at all."

Through expectation, we develop a tunnel vision when we only accept information that supports the view we have of who we want a partner to be. The truth is that people show exactly what they want and who they are through their everyday behaviors. This affects marriage negatively

Marriage entered into with certain expectations, which when unmet or unrealistic, starts and fuels the domino effect which may eventually lead to the end of the relationship. This unrealistic expectation quickly and easily leads to relationship problems. It would be a hell of marriage if both partners are not free to be themselves, to respectfully express their needs and feelings, and to know they are accepted for who they are.

Tips to consider

It is important for both parties in a relationship to take responsibility to mutually express their wishes. The couple must learn how to meet each other's desires and needs, which usually requires compromise on each side. However, individuals may choose to cooperate – or not. If not, the relationship is ultimately doomed.

If the partners agree to compromise, the payoff builds cohesiveness and intimacy. This is the glue that holds the relationship together.

The decision to cooperate is a decision of trust. Trust requires regular communication and sincere engagement with your partner. Once trust is developed, an ease in expressing one's needs and desires to one another can occur. Distrust occurs when one person fails to listen, support, and give feedback. When expectations are not met, trust becomes fragile.

Before each partner can begin to have effective communication, boundaries need to be established. Failing to set boundaries is damaging to the relationship. Remember that there are two separate people in the relationship and it's necessary to assess what is bothering each of them on an ongoing basis. It's imperative that each person knows their limits and learns to discover, and then change, their unrealistic responses. If a person senses an invasion of their boundary by their partner, this is the critical time to verbalize this to them.

When things happen in life, such as traumatic events, people need to learn to readjust and discover new ways to function as a couple. One event affects all other components of life. Successful relationships adapt as changes occur throughout life. There's a rhythm in a relationship. When change occurs, the rhythm is disrupted and may even come to a halt. A crisis creates a test of the relationship. How each individual in the relationship deals with the crisis determines if their relationship will strengthen or collapse.

The key is putting God first in your relationship. We must always allow God's will to be done and believe that bad time will not tarry for long. The couple must learn how to respond to each other, not react. An example that illustrates this situation would be the loss of a child. A possible dissolution of their union may happen if either partner begins to resent or blame the other. One may be too emotional to function while the other may stop feeling any emotion completely If the couple support each other and continue communicating, their relationship can be strengthened.

How to Resolve Expectation
Problems in a Relationship

Recognize the problem

In order to begin the process of redefining and building a flourishing relationship, each person must recognize that there is a problem, be willing to invest their time and energy into the repair process, and accept responsibility by admitting that each party's actions have consequences. The payoff will be a worthwhile investment of their effort.

Listen and be listened to

We each bring our own perspective to any situation, colored by our past experiences and learned behavior. In order for the relationship to thrive, each person must learn to really listen and hear what their partner is saying. It is very easy to get caught up in our own thoughts, and what we are hearing, may be quite different than what is really being said.

A great exercise to incorporate when there is a conflict or misunderstanding is to practice active listening. This requires you to stop the "noise" in your head and focus on what your partner is saying. Each partner should then reflect back on what they just heard the other partner say. It is very helpful to take a deep breath when you are attempting this new approach of listening. This allows you to break the cycle of listening to your own thoughts and, instead, focus on what the other partner is saying.

Develop your personality

Developing a healthier self-image improves and strengthens all relationships. If you are sabotaging relationships, you need to look within and identify what is provoking your misguided thoughts. Focus on the positive, and work toward improving the rest. Suggestions of avenues to explore in developing a healthier self-image are: confide in a trusted friend, look up at Web sites on self-care, consult a life coach, and/or talk to your religious minister. It is essential to acknowledge that we are all valuable and worthy of being loved. Accept and honor yourself as a unique individual. Taking care of yourself means that your feelings, thoughts, and needs are significant. When you find yourself focusing on the negative, stop and take a breath. Let that breath remind you that you are worthy. With each new inhalation, remind yourself you are taking a new step forward in life. You are restoring yourself.

Build boundaries to avoid conflicts

Establishing boundaries is important for an individual, as well as for each individual in a relationship. It is imperative that an individual is clear about defining what he or she considers comfortable and uncomfortable. A boundary is your ability to take charge in all situations of what is acceptable to you. If you feel your partner crosses your boundary, then it is necessary to let your partner know it is not right in a very simple manner.

Your boundary protects you. This means not allowing your partner to attack you with action or words. Once you create your boundary, you will be able to stop any negative or disruptive actions or words from penetrating your boundary. It's like a gate you control who you let in or who you leave out. This boundary is for yourself protection. Example: Rule would be that it is not acceptable to yell when you are angry. Instead, in your relationship, you establish a rule that when one partner is angry, the one who is angry will say "I am angry" "we need to talk about this."

Do not harbor negative thoughts

Couples that have a healthy relationship focus on each other's good qualities and on the positive, rather than drawing attention to their partner's negative traits. This reinforces the continuation of each partner concentrating on the positive aspects of the other person. No matter how much you may love someone, you will not love everything about that person. For a union to be continually successful, it is imperative that each person realistically recognize and then accept the other for who they truly are. This includes your partner's traits that may irritate, frustrate or anger you.

Express your Frustrations and be Patient to hear your Partner's view

When one is upset or angry, lucid communication becomes very difficult. When you are angry, the first thing to go is communication. Blaming and criticizing can become an automatic response if you feel verbally threatened. This can spiral out of control where each person reacts by yelling at the other. When everybody is talking, nobody is listening.

A way to change the communication is to share your feelings, instead of attacking your partner. By using "I" statements, (such as "I feel..,), it allows your partner to hear you without putting up a wall of defense. This way, your partner can assimilate what you have said and respond with their feelings, rather than attacking. This is a much more effective way to communicate than using "you" statements, such as "You always do...."

Speak your mind with humility

By waiting until a later time to express the problem or issue, the emotion is taken out of context. The difficulty of waiting until later is that the other person is put on the defensive. It may be that your partner doesn't remember the event, and time has distanced the feelings that occurred from that prior incident. It may not always be possible to speak up when the feelings occur, but it is a goal for both parties to strive toward. Iron is shaped when it is hot.

What do I want in my relationship?

Nobody wants to initiate the first move, be it pride or stubbornness. Decide what's really important; to be right or to build a quality relationship. This is an essential place to pause and reassess that this is about you as a couple, not just you. This is not the time to gloat or point fingers. The goal is to strengthen your relationship. That is why it is vital to take the first step. Making the first move shows your desire for a happier and more harmonious union.

Learn to compromise

One misunderstanding in an immature relationship is that a person doesn't need to compromise. Once you're in a relationship, it's not just about you anymore. In truth it's now about the two of you. In order to have a cohesive relationship, you have to consider the other partner and their thoughts and feelings. This means verbally discussing the identified issue and then both making an agreed-upon compromise. You need to give at least as much as you want to receive. Change is inevitable if you want your relationship to keep growing.

Take a walk together sometimes

Taking a walk promotes opportunities to discuss your expectations and the desires you have regarding your relationship. Create some kind of initiative that help both of you identify problems and ways to work toward positive alternative.

Develop a "code word" for the health of the relationship

Slip-ups will occur. When either person makes a mistake, such as overreacting to the other, instituting the use of a code word will immediately alert both parties they need to stop and reassess. The code word needs to be decided together. A few examples of code words you could use are: "purple", "circus," "red light" or any word or phrase that alerts each of you in a non-threatening way. Another example is creating a body gesture, as making the letter "T" with your hands to indicate we need a time out. Some Christians use " cross" or " blood of Jesus,".

Where do our problems come from?

List both similar and different values you bring into the relationship-family values and traditions, cultural background, past relationship problems, painful life experiences, political and religious views, and any triggers that set you off.

What hopes or expectations do you have of your mate? Finish the following sentence, "I expect my partner to… This will help illuminate both realistic and unrealistic expectations. Once identified, it is much easier to address and resolve.

Finish this sentence, "I do not agree with your expectations because…" Then discuss ways to reach a compromise.

Answer, and then discuss: "How do you want your needs to be met? Plan a daily time to check in with each other. This creates an opportunity for discussion of any unfinished business or any misunderstandings you need to clear up together. This daily conversation works to strengthen your relationship. It is an excellent tool to use to build more effective communication. A good time to check in could be after dinner or before bedtime. This insures neither of you go to sleep angry or upset.

Finally, having realistic expectations for others involves realizing that all of us are less than perfect. Instead of looking to others to meet our needs, we must take responsibility for our own life.

A fulfilling relationship requires developing realistic and agreed-upon expectations as a couple, where each partner is willing to give to what they want to get. This takes maturity and courage. Accepting and tolerating your partner's needs and limitations requires the same.

When we demonstrate the insight and fortitude to embrace the truth, along with finally putting an end to the pain of constantly being disappointed by unrealistic and unspoken expectations of one another, our relationships have the opportunity to become rich in authenticity, trust, emotional depth. Continual communication is a process. Focus on the positive, and work on improving the rest. All of the tools and strategies discussed in this chapter reinforce the goal of strengthening and nourishing the relationship. This process is most successful if addressed on an ongoing basis, so if you want a healthy and everlasting relationship, please be aware of any expectations.

Chapter 9
The Third Party, Parents and Mentor Factor

The third Party, Parents, and Mentors are the people who are involved in other people's love or marriage relationships. These people contribute positively or negatively to the lives of the people involved in a relationship. They influence a lot and sometimes are made little gods in some couples' lives (especially young couples), because of the roles they played in their wedding. The roles they play in the society, in the couple's wellbeing, and the success they have achieved in their own love life.

The third party factor

A third party is a person who is involved in the welfare of the love or marriage relationship between a couple. Oftentimes, people say that third parties are bad news. They are often the reason for breakups in love relationships and marriages. They are considered pests, rodents, parasites, and weevils in an otherwise perfect relationship. It is not easy to break a strong marriage; however, when a third party shows up, the original couple tends to break up because trust has also been broken through counseling, advice, and gossip. Some third parties end up being involved in sex with one of the couples; some even extort money and mislead either of the couples into extra-marital affairs. So much has been said about the third party factor that some people consider it a taboo in their relationship.

However, I know of one third party who, if allowed involvement in our relationships and marriages, would bring us even closer together, make our love for each other stronger and make our relationships tighter. That third party is God. When we make God the center of our lives, we then make Him the center of our affairs. Just imagine this love triangle--God on top, and we (our spouses and ourselves) at the bottom. The closer we draw to God, the closer we draw to each other. But the moment we draw away from God, the farther away we go from each other toward destruction. A marriage is not perfect. But God's inclusion transforms our relationships, making our love stronger. We become closer and more intimate with each other. If God is at work in our lives, He will also work in our relationships. No marriage is beyond salvation when God works in it.

In my opinion, the existence of a third party is evidence of a relationship under stress. Otherwise, you don't invite someone to come into your sweet relationship. This stress may be from parents, relatives, or friends. It may come from strangers or former lovers. The reasons may be to try to enhance the relationship, persuade one to act in a certain way, or to gain some benefit for the outside person. It may be part of the natural growth and development of the couple, or a turning point toward the ending of the relationship.

Whatever the reason or cause, the stress will alter the relationship unless it can be identified and redirected. Most marriages end in divorce and most people who get divorced say "The person I thought would guide me, destroyed my marriage."

Parent factor

Parental interference in their adult children's love relationship and marriage is a natural and traditional thing. This is far better than the third party factor because so many bloodline issues are involved. Parents who would destroy their own children's marriages do so under the influence of spiritual madness. Parents are parents to both husband and wife, as long as one of the spouses is their adult child. The Bible says the husband and wife becomes one person and both of them should be treated as such by both parents. A couple should be praised in each other's presence and in an open atmosphere. They should be rebuked in like manner. They should be taught how to live together in love, in truth, and also in the joy of openness and transparency. Parents have a very big influence in a couple's lives, in relationships and marriages; sometimes they influence the choices we make in our marriages. Some parents honor this position and do extremely well in their involvement in their adult children's love relationships and marriages. Some parents are as good as the devil too; and their position in their adult children's marriage is evil and destructive. Depending solely on God and relying on good parents is great. Limit bad parents' involvement and interference in your marriage.

Parents will always be parents. No matter how old their children get, there is this instinct in them to have a say in the life of their sons and daughters. The downside of this is sometimes; parents can go beyond their limits and adversely affect their relationship with their child or children and even with their in-laws. It is difficult for parents to be in a situation where family members are not on good terms with one another. Siblings become estranged from one another. Nobody wants this, but sometimes, it can and does happen because of parents' over-involvement.

When family ties get broken due to a parent or a child's action, the break can take years to heal. What happens next is that family gatherings are no longer well-attended as one child decides not to show up to avoid seeing parents or the other sibling with whom he or she had a rift.

Parents should know their limitations. Just because one is

the mother or father does not mean they have the freedom to interfere excessively in their adult child's life and relationships. It's understandable for parents to make an effort to settle conflicts, but wisdom must be applied resolving the conflict in both couple's favor.

Parental over-involvement can only lead to more stress between the couple involved, especially when the involvement is one sided.

Marriage relationships are like families and "siblings relationship," no common personality exists. One will always be different from the other and this difference in traits is often the root cause of conflicts. For some parents, it may be easy to put the blame on one child over the other when something wrong occurs. But in relationship, it's not only one person who's involved and a parent may contribute to the conflict. Parents should respect their adult children's choices for relationships and give advice sparingly and only if asked.

Parents should be polite to their adult child's romantic interests, and even friendly. Parents will have to remember that they need not be the one to fix their child's problems all the time. If your child is already an adult, let him or her experience independence and just be there to serve as a guide. Whether the relationship is with a sibling, friend, or a special person, a parent should think twice before becoming involved in their adult child's concerns. The most ideal way for a parent to give advice is when your adult child asks for your advice. That would be the right time to share your tips and previous experiences with them.

WHY PARENTS INTERFERE IN THEIR ADULT CHILDREN'S MARRIAGES

Parents interfere with relationships for a variety of reasons. In every case, their interference stems from a feeling of entitlement toward the grown child. The parent feels that, by dint of giving birth to and raising their child, they have the right to have some say in their child's life through adulthood. This is not always a bad thing; many times it stops at being mere concern for the grown child's life and gentle, well-meant advice. Unfortunately, in other cases, it goes much further than that. Both parents have the potential for this kind of controlling behavior, though it is generally much more common of mothers than fathers.

Why do mothers interfere?

Misplaced concern for a person's welfare is perhaps the leading cause of motherly interference. In many mothers' minds, their adult children are still children no matter how old they are. The mother has spent the better part of the last couple of decades raising her adult children and advising them in everything, so it's hard to truly grasp that they are now adults capable of making their own decisions and living with the consequences of those choices. If a mother doesn't approve of her child's choice of mate for any reason, she's more likely to try to advise her child out of sheer habit, and often out of a sometimes subconscious belief that she still knows what's best.

From the outside looking in, no one can get a clear picture of any relationship. Many people are content to confide in the importance of each other rather than a parent at all times, except when there's a problem. If there are issues within the relationship, people are more likely to turn to friends or family for advice. Parents are often the natural choice. A person will have had firsthand experience of the kind of relationship his/her parents had and so can see the results of advice given. Many times, parents who have made bad decisions can share with their grown children what they wish they had done instead. However, seeking advice from parents can have the negative effect of making them think that there is more bad than good. When there is no problem you don't confide in them, and when people are perfectly happy they're much less likely to share it with people outside the relationship.

Some mothers see every issue within a relationship as a

confirmation that their misgivings about her child's partner were right. If someone wants to believe something of someone, they are very likely to hang on to the bits of information that support their case and ignore the others. Oftentimes, this is not a conscious thing, but it can lead to very meddlesome behavior on the part of a parent who thinks he or she is working for their adult child's best interest. A parent should work for the interest of the couple.

On the more dysfunctional side, mothers may interfere in a marriage because they themselves are unhappy in their own marriage. For some women, they have never been in a healthy relationship and so are convinced that any relationship their adult child is in will only lead to heartache. They cannot accept that their adult child's happiness is genuine, and so go looking for what must be wrong.

Mothers who have a very clear idea what they want but are not getting it may project their own wants on their children. The result is the constant needling, "Does she do this for you?" "Does he give you this?" and the resultant lectures or disapproval if the answer should be something other than what the parent thinks it should be. Some mothers have difficulty accepting that their children are completely different people and their wants, needs, and priorities will be different.

Finally, mothers with an empty nest may have extreme difficulties giving up control of their child's life. While no one truly has control over another, it's somewhat easier to maintain that illusion when you have the ability to dictate bedtimes, mode of dress, and mete out punishment if the rules are not followed.

This is not to say that all meddling mothers are in any way malevolent or desire to see their children unhappy. In most cases, the intent is quite the opposite. However, mothers are humans too. They have their emotions and imperfections, and sometimes they allow their intentions to cloud their judgment and get in the way of what they are trying to do for their adult children.

Mentor factor

What do we really understand about the word mentor? Understanding the true meaning could halfway solve your problem before you think of getting one. According to the dictionary, a mentor is a trusted advisor or guide in one's life or field. To me, a mentor is someone who is helping you with your career, specific work projects, or general life by giving advice out of the goodness of his or her heart; somebody who wants you to be useful and productive in life; someone to depend on to help you become what you want to be in life, Both good and bad mentors exist. My definition of mentor includes altruism and some sense of "paying it forward" since most mentors have themselves been mentored in the past.

To be a mentor is to have a personality that is considerate and careful; a person who is chosen to guide. In most cases, a mentor has no bloodline relationship with the person mentored. It is always praise for the mentor that somebody has identified him or her as an outstanding personality to have as a guide. This relationship is one of a mutual understanding. The best mentor is God and His word in the Bible. You can have one you have considered so much to be your mentor, but let God be your number one mentor in life. There are times in your life where you will come across someone who gives you advice, makes you feel better about life, and sets you on the right path. You might wonder if that person is a friend, mentor, or both. Here are some thoughts on why you need to distinguish the difference between a friend and a mentor, and why each type of person is beneficial to your well-being.

Friends Have Common Interests

Generally, friendships develop slowly over time because two people share a common interest of some type. Even if their interest is as simple as "trying new cookies", friends develop a relationship by spending time together and pursuing activities they both enjoy. Friendships can be with people of different age groups, co-workers, or folks you meet in a group setting (like church, school, sport center or club).

Mentors Give Advice and Share Wisdom

In a mentoring situation, one person has the advantage in some way, usually with their age and experience level. A mentor has already been through the same situations you are currently dealing with, and they share wisdom based on their experience. Mentors help you at work, assist you in life choices, and gently guide you as you pursue your goals.

You may feel appreciation and even affection for your mentor, but do not assume they are your friend. You may be hurt and disappointed by assuming the status of your relationship.

Mentors Can Become Friends

Early on, a mentoring relationship might feel a lot like a friendship. After all, you may spend time together, enjoy the same hobbies or activities, and have a lot in common. But a mentor generally doesn't become a friend until the two of you are on more equal footing. You will gain experience, and as you do, your mentor will develop a different kind of appreciation for you that will center on the person you currently are, rather than the one you are still trying to be. When that happens, a friendship may develop.

You should be able to understand who he or she is before choosing someone as a mentor. Does he or she have the fear of God? Would your spouse be comfortable with your close relationship with your mentor? How good is your mentor's relationship with his or her own spouse? Your mentor must be a role model in his or her married life. Choosing just any person because he or she is well-to-do, well known in the society, or popular in a certain field is not wise. You need someone who is a good example in marriage; otherwise, he or she may not help your relationship and may, eventually, help destroy it.

Chapter 10
No Retreat No Surrender, in Marriage

"Oh my God! I can't continue in this mess; enough is a enough! It is totally over this time. I got the wrong person for a spouse, God have mercy on me, and I am done". "I divorce you, you divorce me, it is all over now." These frustrating words come out from your heart and mouth because of your inability to love and solve problems as a man or woman. Shame unto you that the stone you rejected as builder, another builder has used it as a 'chief corner' stone. Some people think that there is a perfect mate out there, there is none. Looking for a perfect person in a relationship is an illusion. A perfect relationship can be FORMED by two imperfect people, but perfection in a person can never be FOUND. Love is the labor of two people with two different backgrounds, and up-bringing, two different ideas about life, two different cultures, two different understandings, and two different spirits coming together to build ONE home. From choosing the site, to laying the foundation, and to the finishing of the building, there is bound to be disagreements, misunderstandings, quarrels, and verbal combat between the two. If there was no personal affirmation to stay put by either of them before coming into this union, they will easily break away. But if they did affirm, then there will be room to rethink, reconsider, and reenergize to forge ahead in the midst all the odds. I have nowhere to go, nobody to go to, and you have nowhere and no one to go to. This is all both of us have now, and we have to agree to make it a home comfortable for the two of us.

We have to give and receive, and by His grace, we will be fine. This must be the song of every couple's hearts. A pastor once said. "Every relationship has a cycle. In the beginning, you fall in love with your spouse. You anticipate their call, want their touch, and like their idiosyncrasies." Falling in love with your spouse is not hard. In fact, it is a completely spontaneous experience. You don't have to do anything.

People in love sometimes say, "I was swept off my feet." Think about the imagery of that expression. It implies that you were just standing there. Then something happened to you suddenly. Falling in love is easy. It's a passive and spontaneous experience. After a few years of marriage, the euphoria of love fades. It's the natural cycle of every relationship. Slowly but surely, phone calls become bothersome, if they come at all, touch is not always welcome, when it happens, and your spouse's idiosyncrasies, instead of being cute, he or she drives you nuts.

The symptoms of this stage vary with every marital relationship. If you think about your marriage, you will notice a dramatic difference between the initial stage when you fell in love and a much duller or possibly angry subsequent stage. At this point, you or your spouse might start asking, "Did I marry the right person?" And as you and your spouse reflect on the euphoria of the love you once had, you may begin to desire that experience with someone else. This is when marriages break down. People blame their spouse for their unhappiness and look outside their marriage for happiness and fulfillment. Extra-marital fulfillment comes in. Infidelity is the most obvious, sometimes people turn to work, church, a hobby, a friendship, excessive watching of TV, or abusive substances. But the answer to this dilemma does not lie outside your marriage. It lies within it. I am not saying that you cannot fall in love with someone else but it is wrong and destructive as a married person. Temporarily, you would feel better, but you will be in a worse situation a few years later on.

All couples must understand this one truth: THE KEY TO SUCCEEDING IN A MARRIAGE IS NOT FINDING THE RIGHT PERSON; IT'S LEARNING TO LOVE THE PERSON YOU FOUND.

Sustaining love is not a passive or a spontaneous experience. It will never just happen to you. You can't "find life lasting love. You have to "make" it, day in and day out, to make it last lifelong. That is why I mentioned the expression "the labor of love." It takes time, effort, and energy. And most importantly, it takes WISDOM. You have to know WHAT TO DO to make a lifelong marriage work.

Make no mistake about it. How to remain in love is not a mystery. There are specific things you can do, with or without your spouse, to succeed with your marriage. Just as there are physical laws of the universe, such as gravity, there are also laws for relationships. Just as the right diet and exercise program makes you physically stronger, certain habits in your relationship will make your marriage stronger. It is a direct cause and effect. Know marriage laws and apply the laws, the results are predictable, you make your marriage and love relationship great.

WHAT TO DO TO KEEP YOUR RELATIONSHIP ALIVE

Self-denial and understanding in a marriage

The ability to fear God and make Him the number one person in every decision in your life and totally submit to His will (especially when His will isn't your personal choice) is known as SELF DENIAL. The Lord said that anyone who wants to be His disciple must love Him; surrender to His will, carry his cross daily and follow Him. In marriage, your plans, your life, pursuits are discussed, and agreed upon by both of you. Is no longer "me" but "us and our." Remembering this is a powerful tool in keeping and maintaining any relationship. This unity is the formation of true love and honesty in the life of a couple. The idea to be the "fool" in a committed relationship pays off, and after some time, both spouses become a fool to each other in love. And this is a great foundation of a true relationship. As is often the case, the Bible calls Christians to live spiritually. Instead of pleasing ourselves, we are told to bear one another's failings. Instead of being served, we are commanded to serve. Instead of gratifying our flesh, we are instructed to deny ourselves such gratification. And the moment we are tempted to cry "unfair!" we have only to look upon Christ. Though rightly deserving of gratification, service, and pleasing Himself, the King of kings became a Servant of servants for our sake. He modeled what it means to truly live spiritually by living beyond the dictates of the world. Who are we to think we are above such a life of service if the King has modeled it for us? Love and marriage is a union of selfless and endless kindness and must be carved on our hearts.

Let every discussion be a dialogue that begins, "what do you think, darling?" There is no victory in argument. Let every couple's anger and pain end in love – in kisses, in hugs, and in bed.

The Bible Teaches How to Deny your Self and Make your Marriage Work

Luke 9:23-24: And he said to all, "If anyone would come after me, let him deny himself and take up his cross daily and follow me. For whoever would save his life will lose it, but whoever loses his life for my sake will save it (Terry Ellis & Jerry Rockwell, 2008).

Titus 2:11-12: For the grace of God has appeared, bringing salvation for all people, training us to renounce ungodliness and worldly passions, and to live self-controlled, upright, and godly lives in the present age (Terry Ellis & Jerry Rockwell, 2008).

2 Timothy 3:1-5: But understand this that in the last days there will come times of difficulty. For people will be lovers of self, lovers of money, proud, arrogant, abusive, disobedient to their parents, ungrateful, unholy, heartless, unappeasable, slanderous, without self-control, brutal, not loving good, treacherous, reckless, swollen with conceit, lovers of pleasure rather than lovers of God, having the appearance of godliness, but denying its power. Avoid such people (Terry Ellis & Jerry Rockwell, 2008).

Galatians 2:20: I have been crucified with Christ. It is no longer I who live, but Christ who lives in me. And the life I now live in the flesh, I live by faith in the Son of God, who loved me and gave himself for me (Terry Ellis & Jerry Rockwell, 2008).

Luke 9:23: And he said to all, "If anyone would come after me, let him deny himself and take up his cross daily and follow me (Terry Ellis & Jerry Rockwell, 2008).

Matthew 16:24 Then Jesus told his disciples, "If anyone would come after me, let him deny himself and take up his cross and follow me (Terry Ellis & Jerry Rockwell, 2008).

Romans 8:7-8: For the mind that is set on the flesh is hostile to God, for it does not submit to God's law; indeed, it cannot. Those who are in the flesh cannot please God (Terry Ellis & Jerry Rockwell, 2008).

Jeremiah 29:11-14: For I know the plans I have for you, declares the Lord, plans for welfare and not for evil, to give you a future and a hope. Then you will call upon me and come and pray to me, and I will hear you. You will seek me and find me, when you seek me with all your heart. I will be found by you, declares the Lord, and I will restore your fortunes and gather you from all the nations and all the places where I have driven you, declares the Lord, and I will bring you back to the place from which I sent you into exile (Terry Ellis & Jerry Rockwell, 2008).

1 Corinthians 3:16: Do you not know that you are God's temple and that God's Spirit dwells in you (Terry Ellis & Jerry Rockwell, 2008)?

Luke 4:1-13: And Jesus, full of the Holy Spirit, returned from the Jordan and was led by the Spirit in the wilderness for forty days, being tempted by the devil. And he ate nothing during those days. And when they were ended, he was hungry. The devil said to him, "If you are the Son of God, command this stone to become bread." And Jesus answered him, "It is written, 'Man shall not live by bread alone. And the devil took him up and showed him all the kingdoms of the world in a moment of time (Terry Ellis & Jerry Rockwell, 2008).

1 John 1:8-9: If we say we have no sin, we deceive ourselves, and the truth is not in us. If we confess our sins, he is faithful and just to forgive us our sins and to cleanse us from all unrighteousness.

Galatians 5:22-23: But the fruit of the Spirit is love, joy, peace, patience, kindness, goodness, faithfulness, gentleness, self-control; against such things there is no law (Terry Ellis & Jerry Rockwell, 2008).

Romans 6:23: For the wages of sin is death, but the free gift of God is eternal life in Christ Jesus our Lord (Terry Ellis & Jerry Rockwell, 2008).

1 Corinthians 2:2: For I decided to know nothing among you except Jesus Christ and him crucified (Terry Ellis & Jerry Rockwell, 2008).

Philippians 4:13: I can do all things through him who strengthens me (Terry Ellis & Jerry Rockwell, 2008).

Romans 7:24: Wretched man that I am! Who will deliver me from this body of death (Terry Ellis & Jerry Rockwell, 2008)?

John 3:16: "For God so loved the world, that he gave his only Son, that whoever believes in him should not perish but have eternal life (Terry Ellis & Jerry Rockwell, 2008).

Luke 14:26 : "If anyone comes to me and does not hate his own father and mother and wife and children and brothers and sisters, yes, and even his own life, he cannot be my disciple (Terry Ellis & Jerry Rockwell, 2008).

1Timothy 6:12: Fight the good fight of the faith. Take hold of the eternal life to which you were called and about which you made the good confession in the presence of many witnesses (Terry Ellis & Jerry Rockwell, 2008).

John 15:5: I am the vine; you are the branches. Whoever abides in me and I in him, he it is that bear much fruit, for apart from me you can do nothing (Terry Ellis & Jerry Rockwell, 2008).

John 3:18: Whoever believes in him is not condemned, but whoever does not believe is condemned already, because he has not believed in the name of the only Son of God (Terry Ellis & Jerry Rockwell, 2008).

Luke 18:9-14: He also told this parable to some who trusted in themselves that they were righteous, and treated others with contempt: "Two men went up into the temple to pray, one a Pharisee and the other a tax collector. The Pharisee, standing by himself, prayed thus: "God, I thank you that I am not like other men, extortionists, unjust, adulterers, or even like this tax collector. I fast twice a week; I give tithes of all that I get." But the tax collector, standing far off, would not even lift up his eyes to heaven, but beat his breast, saying, "God, be merciful to me, a sinner." (Terry Ellis & Jerry Rockwell, 2008).

Matthew 5:3: "Blessed are the poor in spirit, for theirs is the kingdom of heaven." (Terry Ellis & Jerry Rockwell, 2008).

Titus 3:5: He saved us, not because of works done by us in righteousness, but according to his own mercy, by the washing of regeneration and renewal of the Holy Spirit (Terry Ellis & Jerry Rockwell, 2008).

Mark 8:34: And calling the crowd to him with his disciples, he said to them, "If anyone would come after me, let him deny himself and take up his cross and follow me." (Terry Ellis & Jerry Rockwell, 2008).

Colossians 1:27: To them God chose to make known how great among the Gentiles are the riches of the glory of this mystery, which is Christ in you, the hope of glory (Terry Ellis & Jerry Rockwell, 2008).

Galatians 3:1: O foolish Galatians! Who has bewitched you?

It was before your eyes that Jesus Christ was publicly portrayed as crucified (Terry Ellis & Jerry Rockwell, 2008).

1 Corinthians 1:30: And because of him you are in Christ Jesus, who became to us wisdom from God, righteousness and sanctification and redemption (Terry Ellis & Jerry Rockwell, 2008).

Romans 8:1-39: There is therefore now no condemnation for those who are in Christ Jesus. For the law of the Spirit of life has set you free in Christ Jesus from the law of sin and death. For God has done what the law, weakened by the flesh, could not do. By sending his own Son in the likeness of sinful flesh and for sin, he condemned sin in the flesh, in order that the righteous requirement of the law might be fulfilled in us, who walk not according to the flesh but according to the Spirit. For those who live according to the flesh set their minds on the things of the flesh, but those who live according to the Spirit set their minds on the things of the Spirit (Terry Ellis & Jerry Rockwell, 2008).

Matthew 6:16-18: "And when you fast, do not look gloomy like the hypocrites, for they disfigure their faces that their fasting may be seen by others. Truly, I say to you, they have received their reward. But when you fast, anoint your head and wash your face that your fasting may not be seen by others but by your Father who is in secret. And your Father who sees in secret will reward you" (Terry Ellis & Jerry Rockwell, 2008).

1 Kings 1:1-53: Now King David was old and advanced in years. And although they covered him with clothes, he could not get warm. Therefore his servants said to him, "Let a young woman be sought for my lord the king, and let her wait on the king and be in his service. Let her lie in your arms, that my lord the king may be warm." So they sought for a beautiful young woman throughout all the territory of Israel, and found Abishag the Shunammite, and brought her to the king. The young woman was very beautiful, and she was of service to the king and attended to him, but the king knew her not. Now Adonijah the son of Haggith exalted himself, saying, "I will be king." And he prepared for himself chariots and

horsemen, and fifty men to run before him (Terry Ellis & Jerry Rockwell, 2008).

1 Samuel 31:13: And they took their bones and buried them under the tamarisk tree in Jabesh and fasted seven days (Terry Ellis & Jerry Rockwell, 2008).

Judges 20:26: 'Then all the people of Israel, the whole army, went up and came to Bethel and wept. They sat there before the Lord and fasted that day until evening, and offered burnt offerings and peace offerings before the Lord (Terry Ellis & Jerry Rockwell, 2008).

Exodus 34:28: So he was there with the Lord forty days and forty nights. He neither ate bread nor drank water. And he wrote on the tablets the words of the covenant, the Ten Commandments (Terry Ellis & Jerry Rockwell, 2008).

James 5:7: Be patient, therefore, brothers, until the coming of the Lord. See how the farmer waits for the precious fruit of the earth, being patient about it, until it receives the early and the late rains (Terry Ellis & Jerry Rockwell, 2008).

2 Corinthians 4:4: In their case the god of this world has blinded the minds of the unbelievers, to keep them from seeing the light of the gospel of the glory of Christ, who is the image of God. (Terry Ellis & Jerry Rockwell, 2008).

John 3:16-17:"For God so loved the world, that he gave his only Son, that whoever believes in him should not perish but have eternal life. "For God did not send his Son into the world, to condemn the world, but in order, that the world might be saved through Him" (Terry Ellis & Jerry Rockwell, 2008).

Matthew 10:37-38: Whoever loves father or mother more than me is not worthy of me, and whoever loves son or daughter more than me is not worthy of me. And whoever does not take his cross and follow me is not worthy of me. (Terry Ellis & Jerry Rockwell, 2008).

Being a boss will never encourage peace and love in your home. Just deny being the boss and the authority but a partner. Never at any time take advantage on your spouse, because two shall be come one and you two are no longer two but have become one person and must live as one in truth and in spirit.

Understanding in relationship

The word understanding looks simple in meaning but is a bit difficult to explain. Understanding means your ability to make a judgment and opinion in an issue or subject. Understanding is the ability to learn something well enough to be able to teach it, make a decision on a matter, and to have the ability to live and associate with others without trouble or a quarrel or a fight.

Understanding is very important in every human relationship, and in every area of human endeavor. Nothing thrives without it. Understanding is one of the most basic needs of a person to live together in a society. Without it, life is very miserable. Understanding simplifies every step toward marriage and every other relationship. An understanding person is humble, gentle, slow to anger and open to others' ideas before making judgment. An understanding person is quick to listen and meditate on what is said.

Understand who your spouse is, how he or she does things, how she relates and communicates, what she likes, and what she hates. It takes time to understand certain things about a person, but it worth giving time. A marriage allows time to learn and understand one's spouse, if it is truly it is, "til death do we part."

Friendly advice

One of the greatest difficulties of being a human is that we can never see what is in the heart, mind, and experience of another person. This is nature's hidden problem in marriage and relationships. Counting on the years of experience, we think we know our partner. We may be partly right, or completely wrong about what our partner is experiencing. That is why it is so important to learn and understand your partner's point of view. A good listener has a great advantage in marriage.

For example, if a wife sighs to her husband, "I am so tired," he may think he knows why she is tired. He may believe that her tiredness is from staying up too late at night. Or he may believe that it is from new demands at her workplace. If, based on his idea of the problem, he gives advice; "Why don't you lie down and take a short rest," he probably will offend his wife. His counsel may be well-intended but not welcome. Most adults don't want advice when they have not asked for it.

What should the husband do differently? When your partner expresses pain, offer him or her support rather than advice. The husband may be tempted to impose his own meanings on his wife's experience by trying to figure things out. Instead he could simply respond to the message she has already given, by saying, " Is there something I can do for you" or "Why are you feeling tired?"

Any effort on the husband's part to open the door for her to tell him more will probably be helpful. She might say, "Everything went wrong at work today," or "I'm worn out when I get home from work" or "I guess I feel pretty lonely." Even with this additional information, a husband is wise to keep listening. Nodding and listening may encourage her to keep sharing. Keep the focus on what she is feeling rather than giving advice or telling her about your experience.

With statements like "I can see why you would feel that way," or "No wonder you feel tired," or "I don't know how you have tolerated it this long." When a partner feels strong emotions, it is a good time to listen and offer support. As the emotions lessen, it may be helpful to ask your partner, "Do you want me to just listen or would you like me to help brainstorm solutions?"

Show love and affection by telling your partner: "I'm sorry you're going through this. I love you." Understanding and the support it conveys are very healing. In fact, there is hardly anything a marriage partner can do regularly that will build a relationship as much as being understanding. Because the pain of others makes us uncomfortable, it is natural that we respond with advice, distraction, or other efforts to minimize the pain. Unfortunately, this prevents the person with the pain from figuring out their feelings and healing from the inside. While it may not be natural or easy for us to respond to pain with understanding and compassion, it can be learned. And it can make a big difference for each partner in the relationship.

How to Present Helpful Advice to a Partner

Talk about your own feelings and experiences as it relates to theirs. For example, " Darling, that same thing happened to me, and this is what I did." One day last month while I was in the office; I sat down the whole day working on the computer. I did not take a break because the workload was heavy. When I was finished that day, I couldn't walk, my chest and my back ached and I was sorely tired.

You must acknowledge your partner's feelings. Let him or her know that you relate to his or her situation, invite more discussion, and shows understanding and supportiveness.

THINGS TO DO ABOUT THE PROBLEMS OF RELATIONSHIPS

Chapter 11
Commitment and Dedication Wrapped with Love

To begin, let us define the word, commitment, to understand its function, in any kind of relationship. Commitment means a willingness to give time and energy to something you believe in, and promise with a firm decision to do exactly that. Commitment requires that you must do or deal with something no matter the cost. This is the meaning of commitment in relationships of marriage and of love. True love in a marriage and in a home makes a relationship beautiful, comfortable, durable and attractive to the eyes of men. It takes the total commitment of both parties to make such a vision into a reality. In marriage and love, building the commitment is not a one-man show. But the man and the woman must be fully committed here. One-sided commitment is a building that will never be built and such a relationship can never succeed.

Commitment is not a one-way street. A relationship is doomed to fail if only one person is committed. Both parties involved should share the same goals, and have mutual agreements on the most important aspects of the relationship. You and your partner should be on the same page, but if you haven't come together to share your views and concerns about the relationship, it will be difficult to be committed in such a relationship.

COMMON SIGNS OF A COMMITTED RELATIONSHIP

Exclusivity

Although some may argue the point, when individuals stop dating other people, reserve their love for each other, and decide to be exclusive, they are signaling their readiness for a committed relationship. It's difficult to establish exclusivity. Nobody really wants to bring the topic into a conversation, especially if a couple has been dating only for a few months. Being exclusive with someone goes unspoken sometimes. The most important thing is that both individuals want to be together.

Long-term Plans

Establishing future plans with your partner is another obvious sign of a committed relationship. After all, to make plans with somebody who won't stick around for a little while seems futile. The more serious the relationship is, the more you will think about your future together. When you tell each other your dreams, it means that you have connected deeply. People who are seeing each other casually will never talk about the future and they focus more on their short-term goals and pleasure.

Giving each other private information

Giving a person your e-mail and Facebook passwords is a big deal. If you reach this stage, it means you two are fully committed to each other. When someone gives you their password, it means two things: They are not fooling or flirting around and they trust you. If your partner still has plans of hooking up with somebody else, there is no way that he or she is going to freely give you the passwords. A couple in a committed relationship does not hide anything from each other. Being committed to a person means not giving them any reason to doubt your intentions. If you want to reach this stage, then do not blatantly ask your partner for his or her passwords and say you need them so you can start trusting. Successful relationships do not operate like that.

Spending the Night

Another obvious sign of a committed relationship is when a couple can't get enough of each other and start to spend nights in each other's apartment. You leave your underwear in his bathroom and he is completely ok with it. He even gives you a room in his closet where you keep a change of clothes. If you start spending the night in each other's places, it means that each of you is making your commitment.

Understand Unspoken Expectations

Couples do things for each other without having to elaborate. If you are attending your cousin's wedding for example, then your man or woman knows he or she has to be there without feeling obligated. When a couple reaches this stage, they tend to feel more secure and they realize that they do things not just to please their partner but mostly out of love. Even though you are in an exclusive relationship, a couple cannot be in a committed relationship until the following occurs in the relationship:

Both of you are actively involved in seeking out each other's company. You are both willing to spend time with each other's family and friends, neither of you are excluded from any area of each other's life. Neither of you have to be alone on special occasions - Christmas, Birthdays, Valentine's Day. Generally, each of you should be able to share gift-giving or signs of affection at these times. Each of you have to offer support when the other has a problem; even if it is difficult, you each do your best. Both of you have to either call or text each other regularly and are happy to hear from each other all the time.

If you have all the above in your relationship, then you can be pretty sure that it meets the definition of commitment. If, however, in the early stages of a relationship, you are having doubts about whether a person is committed to you, then he or she probably is not. This is not necessarily a problem, if you can accept that you just have not reached that stage yet.

COMMITMENT IN MARRIAGE

Spend more time together

A couple spends quality time together. A couple should be together sharing ideas, planning, or doing things together. Apart from the time of being at a job or at a center pursuing his or her career, couples should be together all the time. This gives them time to understand more about each other, discover some good gifts in each other, and plan for their future. Human nature is flexible, if you keep too far from your partner, he or she finds other company.

A couple reassures each other regularly

Communication of love and affection should flow regularly between a couple. There should be no guessing about what is going on inside the other. Commitment in marriage recognizes regular dialogue and collective action on the spoken plans. Expressions of love, plans for the future and kindness for each other's beloved ones must be present in your regular conversation.

A couple should be out-spoken and open to each other

A couple should hide nothing from each other. Speak out when you are in doubt or have feelings of anger, frustration, or disgust. If these couple or partners do not speak out their feeling to one another, it could be easily translated into unpleasant thoughts about a spouse. These thoughts can become something like a grudge in the mind, portraying an image that is carried within you, even when things are going well. The image saps the desire to act lovingly and affectionately toward your spouse. It is a bad pivot which love diminishes. Eventually it can result in an impenetrable barrier to reconciliation

A couple has the intention of being committed to their marriage and spouse. Many also realize that this implies translating commitment into actions. Yet they fail to do it which is to say, that they have never been committed. We must develop honesty within ourselves. There is a human tendency to develop a private logic, or set of beliefs, with which we are comfortable. We avoid seeking the real truth, which can be uncomfortable at times. For example, we feel better if we can believe that the wholesale share of the blame for a problem lies outside ourselves. We may want to believe we can enjoy the independence of single life as well as the unity of married life at the same time. We humans want the satisfaction of being right, innocent, and in control, as well as the mutuality that is possible only when we give these up. Incompatible or faulty beliefs need to be recognized and dealt with honestly, as individuals and as a couple.

We would never consider leaving our children as a solution to our problems with them. If you seriously consider another job, your devotion and performance in your current job inevitably suffers. If your destination is not determined, you are prone to make changes in direction that appear to lead to more interesting or pleasant places. So it is with marriage. Our destination must be the best relationship possible.

If you want your marriage to be everlasting and sweet, consistent with God's design, we must periodically evaluate the nature of our commitment, as expressed through our actions and behavior patterns. True faith is demonstrated in action as well as belief.

Has our commitment to marriage been translated from belief, to intention, to specific behaviors? A sweet relationship is a healthy life.

Commitment is so important in marriages and love relationships. It demonstrates and offer security to all parties involved in the relationship.

DEDICATION

Dedication has almost the same meaning as commitment, but has a great difference to a marriage relationship. In general view, dedication is an official ceremony of opening a building or a place to be used after completion. It is a total surrendering of a place, a person, or property to the purpose for which it is made. It is the complete giveaway to the service of another. Dedication is the state of being committed to someone, a ceremonial beginning of something such as the birth of a child, something written, said, or expressed in honor or in memory of someone. Dedication is a matter of the heart that deals with one's faith and beliefs. There is no victory without dedication.

Words that are synonymous with dedication

Adhesion, allegiance, and attachment, commitment, fidelity, devotedness, devotion, faith, faithfulness, fastness, filthy, loyalty, piety, steadfastness, and constancy.

Look at these words critically and see how they fit in a marriage relationship. Each deals with both physical and spiritual binding in the vow to be together as one person. Dedication in marriage is taking full responsibility for your spouse's welfare. You must be present making sure that his or her physical and spiritual welfare is always in good order. After God is in your heart and service, your spouse is next in line, no matter what happens to be the situation. You are there 24/7 for each other reasoning together, executing plans together, doing everything together. He or she becomes your mother, your father, your lover, your brother, your sister, your best friend, your helper, your gift, your smile, your happiness, your song, your dance, your sleep and dream, your interest, your hobby, your sport, your game, your fashion, your education, your science, your social network, your flirt, your movie and your food and snacks.

You both are for each other. Dedication maintains and keeps healthy marriages and love relationships.

LOVE

According to the Bible, love is the greatest gift of all. As powerful as love is, its strength grows with commitment and dedication. Love has joy, it has kindness, mercy, forgiveness, understanding, and it has life. Love is light. It sees, it talks and it reassures future.

Love does not compromise happiness for money, power, popularity, or fame. All love wants is truth, kindness, faithfulness, and the fulfillment of life and destiny of all. Love is a natural magnetic attraction between two people of opposite sex to share their shame and pride, kindness and happiness in public and secret places in their life. Love is not something we buy, but something we are gifted with. The Bible says that he who finds a wife has found a good thing. Love that depends on material things dies as material things fade. If a love relationship is not founded on love, it is but lust, which has no kindness and no forgiveness.

Just as every building needs a foundation if it is going to stand, so too marriage needs a foundation. It takes significant time and effort to lay a foundation so that the house will not crack and crumble. A marriage is no different. We need to consider what makes a solid foundation in marriage. Love is that solid foundation. Without it, let there be no marriage because the relationship will not withstand a blow.

Nearly 60% of marriages in the United States end in divorce, and of the marriages that survive, more than 50% say they would split up if it weren't for issues like money or children. Moreover, these numbers don't reflect the fact that couples are increasingly choosing simply not to get married at all.

What is the cause of the conflicts that are causing so much unhappiness in these marriages? The answer is obvious: No love. If people become involved in marriages that are not prompted by love, they will definitely continue to get divorced and inflict terrible consequences on themselves, their children, and society.

People all over the world should understand the essence of marriage. No marriage survives without true love, and couples should discover a level of happiness for the health of their marriage. What you give is what you receive; so give love, affection, and reassurance of commitment and dedication to your relationship. Love is the strongest theme uniting all activities in a relationship.

Chapter 12
AVAILABILITY, SHARING AND MONETARY INTEREST

Availability, sharing, both physical and spiritual things in every area of life as well as the ability to be open and equal in administering money is very essential in any relationship of love and marital union. We will look at these words one by one to see their impact in love relationship. First, we look at availability.

Availability

Availability in a marriage relationship means one's ability to be there at any time needed. Availability means an individual making his or her self-present for the physical, emotional, and spiritual use of the other at all time. It is an obtainable access by the other from the other. Availability is the soul of understanding. No marriage will ever be right if the parties involved are not at all times available to each other. Unavailability in a relationship is like strangers meeting and connecting flights at the airport. There is no feeling, deep interest, or understanding about each other. They can laugh and talk a bit, then say good bye in a few hours. You must make yourself available, create the time, be together, have fun, and discuss intimate things for both of you to be fine in your relationship.

MARRIAGE DEMANDS AVAILABILITY

One question which often comes up in relationship work involves how available people are for a healthy relationship. As someone at a recent workshop cried out, "No one today has time for a relationship!" Singles often have a difficult time plugging into a new dating partner's busy lifestyle, and may see their dates as being essentially unavailable for creating a deep, intimate relationship. Couples in a committed relationship may complain that their partner is consumed and distracted by everything about their relationship. They may be around physically, but never seem to want to connect in any meaningful way. Indeed, in our crazy, driven, time-starved world, it often seems as if our adult relationships take the lowest priority.

There are different levels of availability for intimate connection. Physical availability is the most obvious one. Being physically present is no guarantee of intimacy in a relationship, as many married people will tell you. You can be in the same house, or room, or even bed in with someone but still feel very lonely if the two of you are not connected spiritually. However, consistent physical availability is a necessary conductor for deeper levels of intimacy to occur.

The next level of availability is sporadic Emotional Availability. On this level, both spouses are capable of being emotionally present with their own feelings, as well as with the feelings of their partner. The ability to communicate to your spouse what you are feeling is also present at this stage. However, while the capacity for emotional availability is present, the willingness to choose to do so, on a consistent basis, is limited. At this stage, each spouse engages in some form of withholding parts of themselves or in another world of imagination, which results in inconsistent availability. This withholding can manifest in different ways, such as inconsistent time schedules; shutting down or withdrawing emotionally; avoiding difficult topics; or numbing feelings through sports, TV programs, drugs, or work.

The deepest stage of availability is the Conscious Emotional Availability, where the ability to be fully present and mindful of your own emotional process, as well as your spouse's, is present all the time. In this stage, the ability for emotional availability is present, and there is a strong willingness to use that ability. Flow of authentic feelings are acknowledged and communicated on a consistent basis, be it positive or negative. Joy and bliss can comfortably co-exist with sadness and despair, for there is a commitment to each other by sharing the truth of one's experiences with one's spouse.

Why are so many couples unavailable for this deepest stage of human connection? Is the need for relationship no longer fundamental human desire? Why do couples create these complex, overextended busy lives? Why do people fall in love and get married only to be hurt? Why do couples make time unavailable to coordinate their lives together? People want true love but don't make time available to build it.

Many couples and partners think they are available when they really are not. I have seen this demonstrated countless times in intensive discussions. When presented with all the tools, knowledge, support and guidance possible to create more intimacy in their lives, but still they don't build with it.

You must be available. This is really the only solution about availability in relationship. If you are unavailable partners, there is something unavailable in you. You have to be sincere with yourself. You have to create the time if you are really serious. Our relationship with others is but a reflection of our relationship with our inner self. Reflect on what you may be running away from within yourself.

Make a change and promise to be gentle and compassionate with yourself. Begin by becoming fully available to all aspects of who you are. Discover what your fears and barriers to intimacy are, and take steps to remove them. If you find yourself running away or afraid of certain aspects of intimacy, get some professional help from someone who has been down that path themselves. Strip away the barriers to availability and notice what comes up mindfully, consciously, and lovingly. For when you are fully available for conscious emotional connection with yourself, you will attract the same energy into your life from others. Creating and maintaining a healthy relationship is quite similar to creating and maintaining a beautiful garden. If the gardener is unavailable to tend the garden, the consequences are quickly revealed. Similarly, relationships need time and open communication and commitment to weed the inevitable hurts and resentments that occur. Consistent time to devote to a relationship on a physical, emotional, intellectual and spiritual stage is necessary to water the roots of your marriage and love relationship. Like a plant, your love is a living, breathing, organic process that will get stagnant or wither away and die if both of you are not consistently available to keep it healthy.

Committed true love is safe. Not loving is far riskier to human life and health than opening yourself to love. So cancel some of those appointments. Take a deep breath and make room in your life and in your heart for more love to come in. What better use of your time and your life could there possibly be, other than giving and receiving deeper, more committed relationship? You must make the time if you really want to be happy in your marriage and make your marriage sweet and lively forever.

SHARING

Sharing here may look a bit difficult to understand but it is important that we know that sharing is one of the most important factors in a sweet and enduring relationship and especially marriage. Sharing is involved in all aspects of love and relationship. What then is 'sharing?

A dictionary puts it this way: A part or portion belonging to, distributed to, contributed by, or owed by a person or group. As long as there are two people involved in love or marriage, sharing is inevitably present and we must recognize its presence in marriage. In love and marriage, sharing is the ability of couples to divide equally the things they love, the things they eat, things they buy for themselves, the money they have, the time they have, social places they go and even the sex they enjoy.

So sharing is openness, truthfulness, justice and tolerance of all things. Cheating of any form in a relationship is catastrophic; it must be done away with and should never be seen at all. There is no gender advantage in marriage: two have become one and equal in everything they own. Even in sex, when one has reached orgasm, he or she must make sure the other reaches orgasm too; then the sharing is perfect.

Marriages are failing today because folks are busy working on the wrong priority. Weddings are great and fun but do not make any marriage a success. Do not put all your effort in a wedding. People often lose sight of what is important. They put a lot of effort and money into the wedding, only to neglect their marriage in the long run. A wedding is one day, and marriage is lifelong. The glory of one day fades fast, and at some point along the way, couples begin to take each other for granted or work and children take ultimate priority. Suddenly, the marriage begins to fall apart because spouses forget the importance of spending time together.

As love was in their beginning, let every couple try to maintain it in their marriage. Love and marriage can be sweet if you maintain your relationship as it requires. Your life will be longer and your health becomes great too.

HERE ARE SOME THINGS EVERY COUPLE SHOULD SHARE.

Time for Prayer

Couples should share a spiritual life together. They should take time to pray together, and be spiritually grounded. Prayer is the foundation of a peaceful home because there is peace where God resides.

A Bed Together

Married couples should share a bed. For a happy marriage, try to not go to bed angry. No one wants to sleep next to negative energy. Of course, some issues require more time to resolve, but try to release negative emotions to foster a great night's sleep together. These, who order their loved one to sleep on the sofa as punishment need to stop.

Meal Time Together

A couple should find time to share at least one meal together a day. It's a hectic world, but human beings find time for the important things. Marriage should be on the list of important things. No one eats around a dinner table anymore, and little things like this add up over time and cause families to deteriorate.

Sex and Romance

For a single person, I advocate and embrace a life of abstinence, but married folks should be enjoying a lot of sex, lovemaking and intimacy. Give each other massages, rub each other's feet, cook a meal, plan a date night, and wear something sexy or nothing at all. Present yourself as a new person, or up-to-date beauty.

Have Fun

Couples need to take time to reconnect with their happy place. Try a new activity, mingle with others, and by all means, get out of the house. Otherwise, partners become co-dependent and neither will have a life except the one that exists inside the home. Honestly, the word "boring" should never be used to describe a marriage.

Burdens Together

Sharing a burden is hard, but couples need to share each other's burdens. Now, let's not get crazy and pick up burdens we were not called to pick up. That's irresponsible. For example, if one spouse maxed out the credit card, clearing the balance is that spouse's responsibility. People have to be held accountable for their actions, even husbands and wives. All relationships need boundaries and marriages are no exception. On the other hand, if one spouse was laid off, the other has to help in making sure the home continues to run smoothly.

Open mind

The Bible states that, "If a house be divided against itself, that house cannot stand." Couples must operate in one accord, if marriages are to work. They must be on the same page. Otherwise, the household will be in chaos because each person will be seeking different outcomes.

Roles to Share

There are many roles couples should share to make their relationship and matrimonial homes great. These roles (from leadership to household tasks) are endless in a marriage relationship. Couples must discuss and decide who is most competent to do which tasks. Couples must make known their interests and skills, and not base their household responsibility on traditional roles.

Roles vary in different countries, but there is understanding of roles and responsibilities based on personal choices and traditions

Women often take on the role of housekeeper, cook, nanny, dishwasher, dietitian, gardener, tutor, and so on. She is responsible for taking care of the household things and children. Her role is defined around sensitivity and understanding.

Men are often given the role of financial provider, accountant, handyman, referee, manager, and so on. He is responsible for having a career and making decisions. His role is defined around aggression and logic.

The historical definition of roles has created many stumbling blocks in marital homes. Some of these roles were rigid and restrictive, and created a strong division between spouses. This has separated the couple and led to a lack of sharing between them, less intimacy, lower self-esteem, relationship dissatisfaction, more hostility and stress, and feelings of rejection, aloneness and imbalance.

Key Factors for Improving the Quality of Your Role

Remove gender from housework. Talk about and divide housework based on interests and skills rather than on gender.

Work to develop and maintain an equal relationship in terms of power and decision-making.

Keep an ongoing discussion of your expectations and feelings regarding roles and changes you would like to consider.

Sharing is an important in marriage. Two different people have become one person, so what one would want to be done to him is what the other deserves too. There should be no Mr. or Mrs. Do-It-All.

There should be no personalization of properties. Instead of saying, "my car," just say "our car," (our house, our land, our business, our children, our money, our account, our shares, etc.). It is also better to reason together and make decisions and accept gains and losses together, rather than let one carry the blame of a bad decision or investment. Agreement helps make a strong marriage.

MONETARY INTEREST

Money is one of the worst contributing factors for divorces in our society. An individual love of money in marital homes wreaks havoc in relationships. Money is a good answer for almost all physical problems. You must not take what is not yours and you must not covet other people's money. The best way to have money is to work and earn it.

Anyone who has a fair mind about money is a good and honorable partner to have in a relationship. Money has made husbands kill their wives, wives kill their husbands and many divorce their spouses. Futures of many children have been destroyed by the actions of their mother for child support money.

Spouses should discuss their ideas about money. Knowing how they plan to handle finances before coming into the marriage is wise and will make a marriage more successful. Ignoring finances can destroy the marriage.

MARRIAGE WITHOUT MONEY

A marriage without money survives by the special grace of God. It takes both spouses to understand and agree to work to break through the poverty barrier. This is a marriage prompted by true and real love. They know that they need money for:

- **Security**: Money helps you feel safe and secure.
- **Status**: Money helps you create a positive image.
- **Selfless**: Money helps you feel good by giving to others.
- **Targeted Goals**: Money helps you achieve your goals.
- **Spontaneity** Money encourages you to enjoy the moment.

Spouses who know they want to break through the barrier of poverty agree to look to each other to make a difference. They support each other in all levels and grow together. They give and take, and compromise for the needed breakthrough. There is an opportunity to make money, especially where there is love and agreement.

Money can be a primary source of conflict in marriage and relationships, but provides a great opportunity to understand your partner's beliefs, attitudes, and feelings.

Marriage with Money

There is no right way for married couples to manage their money. Management is a science that differs among individuals. There are plenty of wrong ways that money is managed in marriages resulting in mistrust, separation, and divorce. Financial issues are the primary reason for 79% or more of divorce cases in western nations, especially America. It not necessarily the amount of money a couple has that tends to trip them up. It's the differences in their spending habits and especially their lack of transparency and communication.

Husbands and wives with differing financial habits and attitudes can make things work, if they are willing to be honest with each other and willing to bend a bit. For some people, money makes them abusive, rude, disobedient and lawless. They think that money solves all problems and they have no need for fellow humans. Money can destroy a relationship when it stands between a couple. Couples with money still suffer when problems come into their relationships.

Tips on How Couples can Work Together

Decide what you want together

Many people live from day to day. Unfortunately, they also spend from day to day and build no financial nest egg to see them through.

To make progress in saving for the future, approach the future one step at a time. Begin by establishing some short-term financial goals: a vacation next summer or a new car the year after that. A desirable short-term goal can be the carrot-on-a-stick encouragement you need to start a savings plan and take additional steps toward financial security.

Build your future together

As adults, and a couple who will live together for life, you should learn to invest. Invest in long term investments that will yield a good dividend in the future, take some short-term investment risk also. Don't be afraid to invest in your education, skills, and technology. One can't always tell what may turn out to be treasure,

Make a financial commitment to each other and to your marriage

Many people tell themselves that they will begin to save when their income rises, but few ever do. Unless you put yourself first, when you make more money, your expenses will inevitably rise to meet your income, and nothing will be left for you.

Persuade yourself that you deserve to keep a portion of your income for you and your future. Once you truly believe that, make a commitment to set aside 5 or 10 percent of all the money you receive in a special account that's just for you.

Just as some people tithe to church or charity, so you should tithe to yourself. You are worth it.

Learn more about finances together

Most people learn little at home or in school about money, investment, and personal finance. Few people rarely seek formal training in finance as adults. Begin by learning about your personal income and expenses. Find out where your money goes by tracking last year's expenses, and then decide where to changes.

Pocket money

You and your spouse must keep a certain amount of money that you will divide equally if possible; but in most cases you will divide on an equal amount. This money is for your personal transportation, or lunch at work, or giving help to beloved ones and friends. This is the area where most couples become unfaithful and hide some money for these personal little expenses. Each of you should have some money to spend on minor personal needs especially when both couples are not together.

Extended family needs

Both of you have parents and siblings. In your financial plans, make a percentage to support parents and siblings when they are in need. This goes a long way toward making your marriage a blessed one.

Do not hide gifts from your spouse

Every gift you get, make sure your spouse is the first person to know about it. Let every source be made open and known to each other. This dismisses the grounds for suspicious mistrust. Give gifts to your spouse and constantly tell him or her in action how much you are committed to your marriage.

Put the money on the table

Make no mistake in saying how much money you receive. Do not forget some part somewhere. All amounts both of you receive must be spread on the table to be seen and known. Money can cause deceitfulness and must be handled openly in your matrimonial homes.

Do not buy things that are not important

Do not borrow money for parties of pleasure. This may breed disagreement when the time comes to pay it back. Do not buy used appliances, or used clothes because they may not be able to serve you for a long time.

SOME SPENDING GUIDELINES FOR COUPLES TO CONSIDER

Thirty-five to forty percent of your take-home pay is probably spent on housing costs. Ten to fifteen percent goes for food. Your car payment shouldn't exceed ten to fifteen percent of your income. Another fifteen to twenty percent might be spent on variable expenses, such as household repair, recreation, and clothing. Five to ten percent of your budget should go for insurance premiums and property taxes. Five to ten percent of your income should be deposited to your savings.

Start saving

Procrastinators put off saving, or go on spending sprees as soon as they accumulate much of a nest egg. To overcome financial procrastination, begin by setting some minor goals, such as reading one article or newspaper column a week on financial matters. Then add more substantial goals, such as devoting three hours to preparing a budget, and an hour or two a month to monitoring spending.

A couple should work together to develop financial knowledge and confidence. Soon you will find yourself gliding painlessly into the world of finance, and ready to begin your savings plan.

Explore your past financial issues

A couple should carefully examine their early teachings about money to find clues that are sabotaging them financially. As a child, were you taught not to envy those who were better off? Did your family teach you that money is the root of all evil? Was money used to reward or punish in your family? Did you have enough, or were you constantly afraid? As you work to build a financial future together, it is important that each couple understand their deep-rooted attitudes toward money, and the attitudes of their partner. Never buy what you don't need or use, it is a waste of money Reduce conflicts over money matters. That will help you succeed financially in your marriage.

Couples should be balanced in finance

Women sometimes want to control their own lives and make their own choices, while at the same time; they want to rely on others, be comforted and loved, and to provide a nurturing environment for their families.

Men are confused as well. They have been raised to show love and affection through providing financial support. They give it willingly, without due consideration of whom they give it. If a woman does not need financial support, some men are in a quandary: What do women want from them?

Yet if their partner wants to quit her job to take care of the family, they are afraid she will become too dependent on him. This is wrong; no one takes care of your family more than you and your spouse. You both must work it out for the good of the family.

Discuss together the roles that each of you will play in earning, managing and spending money. Talk about how you each feel in the roles you choose, and how money affects your relationship.

Don't shy away from discussing the power and freedom that money brings. Discussing money matters openly will help foster a healthy relationship you both can cherish.

Take action, one step at a time. Some people have no interest in dealing with their personal finances. They know nothing about financial management and how to proportion their interest. Many are always broke before the next paycheck.

For example: If your goal is to amass $100,000.00, it may seem overwhelming at first. But though $100,000.00 sounds like a lot, it's really just $100 multiplied by 1,000.

Money begets more money through compounding. As you seek out ways to create your nest egg $100 at a time, you will become more familiar with the world of money, and that will make it more interesting as well.

Couple should tolerate each other's imperfections

Couple should tolerate each other's imperfections. Do not blame, do not victimize and do not fight about who is right or wrong because the two of you are one.

Some people want to pin down every detail before making any decision about money. But perfectionism delays financial success. Emphasize action: Don't wait until you are fully educated in finance to start saving, or you will never begin. Begin saving now, and then start an investment program using mutual funds.

Making financial decisions creates the possibility of mistakes; it is true. But fortunately, in most financial situations, there are a wide range of right decisions and only a narrow band of decisions that are decidedly wrong.

You don't need to know how to pick the right investment, only learn how to avoid those which do not suit your financial needs.

In a nut shell, money is both a positive and negative factor in great relationships. Let couples stick together in everything, especially in handling money. You will never know the true character of a person until money is spread on the table.

Chapter 13
MARRIAGE COMMUNICATION, WORDS AND HONOR

Marriage communication is the ability to interact, give and receive information between couple. A dictionary defines communication as the act or process of imparting or interchanging thoughts, opinions, or information by speech, writing, or signs. Our interest is the communication couples use in love and marriage relationships. Looking at it closely, communication is how we speak to others and how what is said breaks or builds a connection with them.

Marriage communication

Communication is so important in human relationships that without it, humans cannot co-habit in peace. Communication in a marriage relationship is quite different from the communication obtained in the outside world. In marriage, communication is the force that gives life to the love, and unity shared in the relationship. Communication takes many forms in marital relationships.

Some examples are, Love communication (honey, what do you want for breakfast?), Easy-to-talk-to communication (when we talk, it is as if we have known each other for years), Freedom-in-companionship communication (talking and laughing together without reserve), Tolerance communication (I tell you anything and you never get angry), Calls communication (phone conversation) , Comfort communication (whenever you talk to me, I feel inspired), Social communication (Facebook discussion, clubbing, etc.) and Easy-access communication (someone you reach to with protocol). All of these help build a sweet and happy marriage.

Most couples fail to communicate effectively because they do not fully recognize the importance of communication. Messages between spouses are often misunderstood and sometimes not even received. Intentions are not clear. Issues and meanings are misinterpreted. Every day, husbands and wives react to each other like stranger. Struggling to find ways to talk to one's better half shouldn't be so stressful.

People marry when they are in love, and any marriage that is not founded on love will not be a happy relationship. A couple in love marries because they want to spend the rest of their lives together. They have every hope of growing together and creating a lasting relationship that is emotionally healthy. To achieve this goal, they have to pay great attention to the skills of communication because communication is the key to a successful marriage.

Love and desire open the flow of communication levels. A couple shares general information, facts; opinions, and beliefs; feelings, emotions, needs, intimate concerns, hopes, and fears. So the key point is sharing your mind with your spouse at no cost and no stress.

Nowadays however, people are self-centered and usually neglect the value of communication, and its importance in relationships, in marriages, on the job, and in all aspects of our lives. A couple may get into trouble in their marital communication because they have not developed their ability to listen and communicate in sweet love manner. This prevents a spouse from communicating effectively: not knowing how to communicate properly; not taking the time to think through what they want to say; not taking the time to anticipate what their partner might be thinking and feeling; fear of revealing too much of themselves; fear of their partner's anger and not wanting to hurt their partner's feelings. These are barriers to a sweet relationship.

Love communication

This is a way lovers and couples smile and laugh while talking to each other. There is a way they look at each other, touch each other, and approach each other when they want sex. They give each other special nicknames that make each other feel made for the other. This kind of communication is instrumental in building a sweet love and marriage relationship. If this love communication does not exist between spouses, their relationship is not based on love.

Easy-to-talk-to communication

Love makes a lion a pet. No matter the age difference, a couple finds it easy and sweet to talk to each other, easy to understand each other, and easy to forgive any wrong. You do not need any protocol to talk to your spouse; you do not need to plan a speech, a format or particular time to talk to your spouse. You confide in each other, and share feelings and burdens. No matter how angry and hurt you are, you are comforted by his or her presence and words. You enjoy listening to each other. Make sure you are easy for your spouse to talk to. It makes your marriage a celebration.

Freedom-in-companionship communication

When there is no comfort in the company or presence of one's spouse, there is a problem. Each spouse must be free to talk, laugh, ask questions, and be well-desired in each other's presence. This freedom must be part of the marriage; otherwise, one spouse is ruling the other; which does not favor a marriage at all.

Phone (call) communication

There is no limit to calling your spouse to find out how he or she is doing, feeling, and if there is any way he or she needs your help. So many people fall in love because of this type of communication. It demonstrates caring, being concerned and sharing love. The more you call your spouse, confide in each other, the more you become intimate and the more the relationship grows Call each other at every little opportunity you have, find out what you can do for him or her, ask if he or she is safe, or you can just say, "I love you, I appreciate you, darling." You can call to say, "I am just thinking of you, I wonder what I would do in life without you," and many more words of love.

The tolerance communication

No matter how good and civilized an individual is, a trace of habit makes him or her different. Every spouse must overlook those little bad habits and reforms those bad habits gradually in love and humility. We all are unique with individual issues of life. Tolerate the bad habits of your spouse, and your spouse will tolerate your bad habits as well.

PROBLEMS OF COMMUNICATION IN MARRIAGE

It is because the couples may have different backgrounds, perspectives, personalities, and professions. Some couples may keep misunderstanding all inside to avoid the confrontation, but that does not make the relationship any healthier. Couples need to find an effective method of communication. Couples must learn to understand each other better and recognize and accept each other's point of view.

How to be a good communicator

You should know a few required communication skills. First, bear in mind that verbal ability is a beautiful gift, but it can turn ugly if abused. There are some communication firecrackers that you must not throw in your argument, or they will spread and intensify the conflict and make things even worse. Besides, active listening is a way of communication in marriage that creates the important climate of acceptance and understanding. Active listening is a valuable skill because it demonstrates that you understand what your partner is saying and how he or she is feeling about it. Actively listening does not mean agreeing with the other person. The point is to demonstrate to your partner that you intend to hear and understand his or her point of view. This is good for your relationship. In addition, an apology is a special way to demonstrate your empathy and acceptance. A person may be sincerely apologizing and yet, the apology is not perceived as sincere because it is spoken in the wrong tone. The five distinct languages of apology are: expressing regret; accepting responsibility; making restitution; genuine repentance and requesting forgiveness.

Learning to effectively communicate in marriage is one of the most important aspects of any relationship. To some extent, effective communication is something that can be taught. Learning to handle confrontations through communication in marriage is an art, like learning to dance. You should know the basic steps to master the dance of communication. It is also something that should come from the heart. Effective communication takes practice. Learn it and apply it daily in your marriage.

VALUES IN MARRIAGE OR LOVE RELATIONSHIP

Values are important elements of tradition that add harmony to relationships. One's values will surely lead a person into a successful relationship. One can work with values and succeed, or work without value and fail.

Important Values in Marriage

Marriage is considered one of the most sacred institutions of life. Those who believe and have applied it in their marriage relationships never regretted doing so. Sadly to say this, there are no perfect people going into marriage in this world and there is no such thing as a perfect marriage. Marriage is a union of two imperfect people striving together to make a close-to-perfect relationship, so it does have a few flaws. The marriages that do work are based on certain values. African marriages survive more because of these values.

Honesty of Partners

Honesty is one of the most important values in any relationship, but most importantly in marriage. It is the basis on which all other values stand. The two people involved should be honest to each other about the relationship. Anything done or acquired in dishonesty disappears quickly, and in most cases they disappear leaving behind on the dishonest person a scare of shame and disgrace.

Equality of the couple before their in-laws

Equality in partners' status is important. Most parents often put the welfare of their own adult child first and do not care about their son-n-law or daughter-in-law. This is wrong and can cause division between the couple. Husband and wife are equal and have become one person before God. Neither one is greater than the other, nor should parents not incite either of the couple to feel more important than the other. Most marriages end up in divorce because one of the partners does not think of his or her spouse as an equal. Husbands often think that caring for the children is the responsibility of the wives, and wives often think that it is a husband's job to be the bread-winner of the family. Unless and until you start thinking of your significant other as an equal to your spouse in all aspects, you will have problems in your marriage.

Commitment to God, Parents and Each Other

Commitment is the most important value in any marriage. When a couple is committed to the word of God in their beliefs, they would choose to never disobey God's word about the marriage relationship. Spouse should be committed to do God's will and honor their both parents. They must set a quality standard on their relationship. Lastly partners should be committed to the relationship equally and never do anything to create difference in the couple's

Respect for Parents and Partner

Respect is one of the most important values in a healthy relationship, Respect increases when you give it to others. You simply cannot expect anyone to respect you or your point of view if you do not do the same for them. Each couple must have a great respect for their spouse's parents and siblings. Respecting the people your spouse respects makes respect a family value.

Discipline

Everyone has much responsibility. One is responsible for parents, siblings, and livelihood, but the manner in which one carries each responsibility is the discipline. These responsibilities can also reform one to be disciplined in all efforts. It is a common notion that being disciplined is to do your work in a routine fashion. It is not just that. Discipline requires one to learn how to best understand people, and offer the support and encouragement to people in life and fulfill one's vision.

Appreciation

Everyone has the spirit to appreciate those who make them feel important. You appreciate God for your life. You appreciate your parents for bearing you and caring for you into maturity; you appreciate your employer for your livelihood, and the list goes on. In this same manner, you have to appreciate your spouse for loving you, for sharing life with, and being there for you, and for committing to you. Learn to appreciate whatever your spouse does.

Giving gifts

It is better to give and be thanked, than to receive and say "thank you," all the time. Giving makes you look great and respected. My mother used to say. "That those who give, never lack because God gives to them." So they keep on giving to those in need. Giving is a demonstration of love and there is no better way to say "I love you" than giving your spouse that which he or she cherishes from time to time. Spouses should make gift giving a tradition in the matrimonial home. God loves a cheerful giver.

Outing

Going out once in a while is a great way to enjoy love. To enjoy a relationship to the fullest, your spouse wants to be seen with you, wants to be proud of you, and wants to let the world know that his or her life is full of happiness. Dancing, watching sports, and going places to have fun make life fast, lively, and interesting. Stagnant water smells, move around and have fun together.

HONOR IN MARRIAGE

Hebrews 13:1–6

Let brotherly love continue. Do not neglect to show hospitality to strangers, for thereby some have entertained angels unawares. Remember those who are in prison, as though in prison with them; and those who are ill-treated, since you also are in the body. Let marriage be held in honor among all, and let the marriage bed be undefiled; for God will judge the immoral and adulterous. Keep your life free from love of money, and be content with what you have; for he has said, "I will never fail you nor forsake you." Hence we can confidently say, "The Lord is my helper, I will not be afraid; what can man do to me" (Terry Ellis & Jerry Rockwell, 2008)?

The Bible is the manual of life. "from conception to death and eternal life is the Bible" "Genesis to Revelation." The Bibles says, God honors marriage and gives favor to them who are involved in it. Any marriage that has no honor is a death trap union. Laws govern every area of human endeavor; and in marriage, honor is the law. Ignorance of the law is no excuse. The punishment is there to fulfill the existence of the law; and in this case, it is God's punishment. You must observe honor in your marriage, honor for your spouse, and honor for the things you share: your body, your bed, your word, your hangout, your friends, your job, and your social actions. When honor is in your marriage, your relationship is safe.

In the beginning God created man male and female in his own image, and he blessed them, and said "be fruitful and multiply" and fill the earth . . . . "Therefore a man leaves his father and his mother and cleaves to his wife, and they become one flesh" (Genesis 1:27–28; 2:24). This is the glory of the precious and honorable reality called marriage: one man and one woman cleaving to each other alone in covenant commitment and one-flesh sexual union until death separates them.

Do not commit fornication or adultery (we human beings are stubborn) we do commit all.

The way to honor marriage is to not commit fornication or adultery. That's what the second half of the verse says: "Let the marriage bed be undefiled; for God will judge the immoral and the adulterous." The word translated "immoral" means those who commit fornication in distinction to adultery. Both actions dishonor marriage and defile the marriage bed. Adultery and fornication, both commit the same evil: having sexual relations with someone who is not your lawful spouse. It's called adultery if you are married; it's called fornication if you are not married.

Both adultery and fornication dishonor the marriage relationship and defile the marriage bed. God made marriage, and marriage alone, as the one holy, safe, and ultimately, joyful place for sexual relations (1 Corinthians 7:2). The text says that God will judge fornicators and adulterers because they dishonor marriage and defile the marriage bed. In other words, God's judgment falls on unrepentant people who destroy what is meant to be a sacred covenant relationship. Repentant" leads to another way to honor marriage and keep the marriage bed undefiled.

LIVE OUT FORGIVENESS AND JOY AND HOPE

We honor marriage when we live out a clean and happy future after our unclean and forgiven past. The text says, "God will judge fornicators and adulterers." Just like 1 Corinthians 6:9–10 says that "fornicators and adulterers will not inherit the kingdom of God." But then the very next verse says, "And such were some of you. But you were washed, you were sanctified, you were justified in the name of the Lord Jesus Christ and in the Spirit of our God."

Hebrews 9:27–28 So there is judgment on fornicators and adulterers, but not all of them. There is escape from judgment for some. Hebrews teaches this message very clearly. In Hebrews 9:27–28 it says, "Just as it is appointed for men to die once, and after that comes judgment, so Christ, having been offered once to bear the sins of many, will appear a second time, not to deal with sin but to save those who are eagerly waiting for him."

So you can see there will be a judgment. But Christ has borne the sins of many—He has taken the judgment for their fornication and their adultery upon himself. And now He is coming, not to do that again, but to save us from the final judgment.

Look at Hebrews 10:12–13, "When Christ had offered for all time a single sacrifice for sins (for fornication and adultery), He sat down at the right hand of God, then to wait until His enemies should be made a stool for his feet. So again you see two things: Christ took sins like fornication and adultery upon himself and paid their penalty in his own death. But there is coming a time when His enemies will be made a footstool for his feet. There is a judgment.

So what we see is that there are two groups of people: those whose sins are covered and forgiven by Jesus (Hebrews 8:12: Hebrews 10:17–18), and those whose sins will come down on their own heads in the judgment. The difference is in turning from sin and coming to God through Jesus for forgiveness and help. Hebrews 7:25, "Jesus is able for all time to save those who draw near to God through Him."

Do not do anything that will damage the trust and commitment you share with your spouse because once this happens, your marriage is no longer an honorable and trusted marriage. Prevention is easier than the cure.

Chapter 14
Sex, Mood, and Sex Presentation

This is the chapter where we have to break the fallow of relationship problems and hit hard. If it is not money, then it is sex that breaks up the majority of relationships and marriages. Sex is not just what we call it, or the way we look at it. Sex involves every factor of relationship. It is physically and spiritually a complete demonstration of true love. It is through sex that you can differentiate true love from fake love. The mouth can lie, actions can be deceptive, or manipulated, but the look of love in another's is genuine and never lies. There is no need to define sex here; instinctively, everyone knows it. Love relationships and marriages begin to fail if sexual energies are not fully harnessed. It is not just thrusting the pestle into the mortar and pounding. So many are things involved; that is why sex is an "ART" which you need to design and paint beautifully, and a SCIENCE to be studied and discovered.

Sex is a serious matter, because it sets true lovers and couples apart from the rest if well harnessed. It ruins marriages and love relationships if not properly enjoyed. You may think being a muscular man is an advantage in sex, but, it is not. You may think having a huge or long male organ (penis) is the secret or buying and taking enlargement pills is an advantage, it is not. What God has made,

He has made and it is good. On the other hand, you may think that women with flat buttocks do well in sex. No, they do not. You may think that a woman with a great shape is good; you may think that women with deep vaginas are great in sex, but they are not. The truth is that sex is the natural inborn, creative ability and exploring mind of a person to know more than what he or she thought she knows. Many lovers and couples never take the time to explore, or investigate what make sex the sweetest thing couples can enjoy. Perhaps they are shy or they do not want to be looked upon as an immoral person; but for some reasons known to them, they retreat physically and spiritually and become dead to sex. What sets into a relationship after that is silence, malice, gossip, quarrels, and fights?

So many couples would have stayed married and taken care of their children if they had idea of what sex is all about. We will discuss here all you need to do about sex that will keep you a happy couple all your life. Some people say that they do not like sex or have no feeling for sex any longer, when they are still not eighty years of age. They say this because they are fed up with their routine pattern of sex, or they do not know anything about sex or they could not work out anything that would help, so they conclusively say there is nothing in it. They need help and that is why this chapter is included.

It is true that as your relationship develops, sexuality changes. This is normal. Since intense sexual attraction is usually an important bonding element early in relationships, sexual changes often seem unwelcome. Lovers or couples become numb, dull and unprogressive. A wife no longer updates herself, takes on the look of a maid; some make themselves look like old women or unkempt widow. Many factors are involved in these changes, but you must not accept this change as something normal.

Before we talk any further about the challenges of sex in marriage, it's worth noting that married women and men report being significantly more satisfied with their sex lives than either single or cohabiting people because they do not remember the law of variety.

One of the most fundamental challenges is the decline in sexual novelty. Novelty is a major sexual stimulant. Novelty is automatic early in your relationship. Later, sex naturally becomes more familiar and less novel with your partner. Low desire is the top sexual problem in marriages. (For men, the top complaint is low frequency--although many women share this concern; for women, the top complaint is quality.) You may need to seek approaches to increasing the stimulation of your sex life at some point to compensate for the loss of partner novelty. The basic strategy is to seek new sources of novelty and variety. Other common interfering factors include anger, time, avoidance and anxiety.

While most couples do not want to make love while they are in the middle of a fight, it's a mistake to put aside your sex life for an extended period because of disagreements, Volatile couples, especially, may find making up from fights to be a passionate experience. Repair your fights and do not interrupt your sex life out of anger. Sex starvation should not be used as punishment for wrongdoing. This could stir up unfaithfulness.

Lack of time is one of the most often cited reasons for infrequency of sex. One of the most common myths is that sex has to take a certain amount of time. Of course, leisurely sex can be wonderful. But it's a luxury that few couples can afford on a regular basis. If you wait for a big chunk of time and the right mood for most sexual encounters, your sex life will become infrequent if your life is busy. You have no excuse but to make the time.

Another top myth is that sex must be spontaneous. It's a fact of modern life that we plan and schedule everything that is a priority. Make sex a priority and include it in your schedule. Date night is popular with many couples, but day time sex is important because variety also make a great difference. Some couples often avoid sex because their sex life has become dissatisfying or conflicting. Talking about it is uncomfortable, and for most couples, it is. Avoidance can become their only chance of least resistance. Lack of time is often a convenient excuse. Talking about sexual concerns in a caring way and planning together for sexual revitalization can be the cure for avoidance.

Anxiety is another frequent interfering factor. Sometimes anxiety is related to inhibitions acquired earlier in life. Performance is another big source of anxiety. Performance used to be a male concern, but now women, too, feel pressure to perform sexually. It is hard for mere human beings to live up to the sexual expectations and ideas promoted by the media, but sex is an important bonding component in marriage. Even if you feel somewhat alienated from your partner, sex can often be the experience that restores your relationship. It can allow you both to feel closer, get affection and stimulate a sense of intimacy. For some men who don't talk very much in relationships, sex can help them open up a little. From a biological point of view, sex has a very positive effect on brain chemistry that can make an important contribution to the ongoing health of your marriage. Sex primes the pump for intimacy and healing in marriage. Marriages that do not maintain their sexual vitality are very much at risk because sex is the only thing that makes two people feel real intimate and as one person. Plan together to protect and promote your sex life as you read this book.

SEX AS AN ART AND SCIENCE

There are many aspects of sex to discuss here, so that you and your spouse will understand and also know how to handle it. These aspects are: Sex as food, sex as medicine, sex as rest, sex as restoration, sex as adventure, sex as exercise, sex as birthday, and sex as joyful event. Discover these aspects of sex and bring them alive into your relationship.

The art of sex has more than a physical requirement. It also needs depth in mutual understanding, emotional attachment, warm feelings of caring and sharing for the spouse, erotic synchronization and true intimate love between two persons of opposite gender. The art of sex is not a time-bound activity. It is, in actual fact, a process of taking yourself and your partner to the height of heartfelt delight. The sole purpose of engaging in sex, apart from making children, is to enjoy it mutually with your spouse.

There are still millions of married people around the globe, male spouses in particular, who just take sex as a pleasure-oriented ritual. They do not care about whether their soul-mates (partner) also enjoy the same level of that physical union as they do. Their primary focus is initiating intromission, as soon as two nude bodies touch each other, to achieve orgasm. They do not understand the essence of the art of sex in marriage. You must use what you have to create pleasure, make it your business to make your spouse happy and reach climax. It is what you do, how and why you do it: how you touch, talk, kiss, screw, twist, pump, suck, and groan. It doesn't matter if your organ is big, long, or small but, how you use the organ that you have that makes the difference.

Marriage is a journey that takes a couple down every single track of life; whether it is social, financial, personal, or sexual, they are together. Sex is one of the most important activities of a marital relationship. The art of sex is a combination of techniques, physical gestures, creative movements and a mutual desire to experience gratifying contentment. You do not have to be a qualified sexologist to learn the art of sex. Simply adopting and practicing the following hot tips can bring a sensational change in your sex life.

Be patient and avoid early intromission

Two exercises are very useful in building stamina: Sit-ups for men and Kegel exercises for women. Both help delay orgasm and make your sex more thrilling and rocking.

Prolong foreplay and delay genital caressing

The art of sex begins with foreplay that is gentle and more

sensational and enjoyable in the whole episode of sex. You can enjoy every moment of foreplay provided you stop focusing on orgasm. Every part of the human body, both male and female, has certain hot spots which erotically react to kissing and soft touching. Try brushing kisses on erogenous zones before indulging in full kissing. Depending on the structure of the tissues of your lips, you can experiment brushing kisses on the whole body of your spouse or just on erogenous zones. The sizzling effect of a prickling tongue smoothly massaging your spouse's body creates waves of incredible sensation through your own body. Use fingertips for soft caressing. Instead of using the entire hand; try soft caressing with fingertips that also radiate stirring currents of erotic energy.

Do not skip a tongue massage during foreplay

Another gigantic feature of the art of sex is tongue massage that runs from face to toes, using both the tip and the whole of your tongue. Performed after showering together, it is like adding more spices to a pasta dish. I strongly suggest avoiding extreme oral sex during tongue massage. You can create many new body gestures to allure and appease your partner during foreplay, making it a cherished experience for days and weeks. The only important factor in enjoying foreplay is synchronization of movements. It should be reciprocal to keep the fire continuously kindled.

The art of sex has no fixed limits and it is not worth much consideration as to where to start the foreplay. Just follow your emotions, your moods, and the nature of ambiance which you have either created or are in by chance. It is advisable to have in-depth talks about foreplay that would also enhance an erotic rapport between both of you. Sex is such a powerful ritual in relationship that without it marriage is nothing but having a roommate.

SEX IS SCIENCE

Every day people discover new and interesting formulas for and news about sex. Anything that has no definite formula, but involves research and discovery is a science. Couples take their time to discover the erotic parts in their spouse, how to prolong orgasm, how to position in sex. People discover how to use drugs and pills discovered and produced by doctors to enhance sex. People discover how to hold their partner to make him or her feel long-lasting pleasure. All this researches and discoveries make sex a science.

As I mentioned above about the sex accepts, we have to look at each of them and see how to use them to restore pleasure and happiness in marriages and love relationships.

Sex as food

Everyone eats food to stay alive. When you are hungry, you do not need someone to tell you that you are hungry. You know and desperately you reach out for food. Even a child, who has not started to talk or walk, cries hungry. Food is good for good health, growth and most importantly food is vital for life. Those who do not eat well are always sick, they have no stamina, they have no fine body texture, they do not grow well and they do not live long. People, who have little food or do not have much to eat, steal food when they see it, or eat anything given to them. They do not care if it well prepared or prepared in a hygienic place, they just eat to end hunger.

As food is to the body, so is sex to human beings' natural desire. This is a fact: When the body wants to have sex, it naturally compels you by secreting the hormone that causes you to go out for it. When a spouse is well sexed in marriage, he or she does not engage in extra-marital affairs because he or she has enough of sex at home. When you sex regularly with your spouse at any time you want it satisfactorily, with exploration, and adventure, any sex proposed to you outside the one in your marriage, seems dirty and unclean. You don't desire it at all and you fear getting an infection. There should be no holiness or righteousness in bed with your spouse. Explore, making sure both of you reach satisfaction and experience every desire, and feeling before you stop. When you are starved for sex, then the intention to cheat or engage in extra-marital sex becomes real.

A female counselor in Africa, used to tell me, "Jeremiah, I am seriously tired today," So I asked, "what happened?" She would say, " I sexed the whole night long. Yea, the vagina is made to be sexed and properly sexed and that's what I do," she joked. We laughed, but that is how it is supposed to be. When you starve your spouse of sex, do not cry when she or he begins to cheat. When you deny your spouse sex, do not think you are still married; you have already divorced. A child who eats well at home does not lust after the neighbor's food. Once a spouse steals sex from outside, he or she will continue to do so because something you hide and do in hurry never satisfies.

Sex is a medicine to the body

A friend from Africa used to say, "Women are men medicine", and I would respond, "Men, too are women's medicine." Some years ago, a psychologist told my friend who was confused and had a hard time sleeping at night that he needed a wife with whom to spend time and have fun and he would get well. Indeed, when this guy got married, all little sicknesses and sleeplessness in his life disappeared and he became well. At one time in my life, I was having constant abdominal pains, and I went to the hospital. After my examination, the doctor told me to have sex. For more than two years at that time I abstained from woman. Abdominal pain disappeared when I started having sex.

It is hard to believe, but it is true - a lack of sex when you are an adult can complicate your mind. Lack of sex can make some women have irregular menstruation and abdominal pains too.

IMPORTANCE OF SEX TO THE BODY CHEMISTRY

Sex rids the body of worry

Sex helps the body to relax and reduces the mind from worries. The moment couple or partners are engaged in sex, their body chemistry change, their minds change focus from worry to pleasure. At this time, couple no longer think about problems but concentrate on the momentarily pleasure, their minds rest and they feel at ease. I discovered that sex reduces worries and revive the body when I was in Sierra Leone during their rebel war. Couples were having children even while they were taking refuge in the bush. They told me they use sex to reduce their worries and look up to God.

Sex burns fat (calories)

Sex is a kind of labor every grown normal individual physical engages without really knowing he or she is laboring. In real sex, no matter how cold the venue is, the partners perspire and sweat. Thirty minutes of active sex can burn off a good amount of fat or calories off from the body. The more couple or partners engage in sex, the more calories they burn off from their bodies weekly.

Sex improves heart condition

Naturally, when people get into sex, their hearts bits increase. In excitement, some people scream to catch up with their breath, their blood circulation runs faster and this action keeps the heart in a kind of exercise for heath reason. This kind of exercise helps cleans and clears blockages and clotting from the blood stream.

Sex makes one feel good

People who satisfy their partners in bed always feel good about their self and wanted by opposite sex. This kind of feeling gives confidence and attracts respect from the partner. Unlike the opposite who can not sex well or satisfy her or her partner feels incomplete, weak and ashamed. So sex improves individual self esteem.

Sex reduces anger

It is true when couple has misunderstanding and they follow it up with sex, their anger dies down and reconciliation begins. Sex is settles anger and introduces peace in a situation, it restore relationship. Some people instinctively get into sex when they are angry. Sex calms people down for reconsideration.

Sex gives concentration

An auto-mechanic told me that he finds concentration in sex. Whenever an auto-repair gives him a hard time, he defers the job for the following day and when he gets home in evening, he just makes sure he has good satisfying sex. The following day he fixes the job with ease. He gets full concentration and transmutes the sex art to his job.

Sex as rest

Good sex really does make a couple weak after they have fully enjoyed and exhausted themselves in it. This weakness sends them into deep sleep, thereby creating a great opportunity for the whole body to rest. Good sex rests the mind, the organs, and even the heart.

Humans spend one third of their life sleeping. This one third has significant effects on their waking life, in terms of productivity, energy, alertness, creativity, memory, body weight, mood, safety, and good health. I urge you to have pleasurable sexual relations at least once a week before bedtime. Researchers have found that this can promote sleep onset and induce deep and restful sleep.

Sex as restoration

Every man on earth is created the same, but the difference in every man created is the state of his heart. If the heart of a man is joyful, there is hope in that man's life. My research shows that there are three major factors that make a man's heart joyful. They are: wealth, health and sex. Sex restores joy to the heart, sex restores unity, sex restores confidence, sex restores love, and sex restores strength. A relationship that is sexless is unhappy, untrustworthy, and unsafe. Sex is restoration indeed.

Sex as adventure

Life is an adventure. For a man's life must be fast, sweet and interesting, he must venture into the deep secrets of life. Sex is one of these secrets. Sex has the immense power of giving a whole U-turn to the attitude we have toward living, especially in married life. Anything routine becomes boring, so you will enjoy sex more with your spouse or partner by discovering new patterns and styles. A woman, in most cases, adores such a partner and will never back off from such a man. Work hard and do something new every time you have sex. Make sex great and discover something that excites you each time you engage in it.

Sex as exercise

Sex is an exercise in which you do your best to make the body become active and flexible. Twisting your body and trying all kinds of positions to enjoy maximum pleasure, sweating, panting and screaming are good for your health. Sex is one game in which we exercise to stay fit, reduce stress, and induce deeper sleep. Exercise elevates body temperature, and an ensuing drop in body temperature at bedtime will induce drowsiness and deeper sleep.

It is very common for couples who are married for quite some time to feel that sex is no longer an enjoyable activity but a routine.

So how can couples spice up their sex after marriage? One of the best ways to spice up sex is to try out different exciting adult games with your spouse. Good adult exercise can prolong your foreplay which is definitely a must if you and your spouse want to experience a better love-making session. This is the best game you can play and make a great difference in your marriage. Massages and touching do enhance sex performance. Try it to whet your appetite.

Sex as birthday

Children always look forward to their birthdays with excitement and plan to make it a memorable one. They think about it all season, plan and find ways to get money to celebrate it. This is how it is with sex. When you have a date or you have agreed with your spouse that tonight will be the night, you look forward to it with happiness and excitement. Some people want the hour to come quickly, and some people find themselves thinking about how great it will be. It makes their day.

Sex is created by God. Sex is holy; sex is good, it is meant to be enjoyed in a marital setting. Sex is not evil .Sex outside its purpose wreaks havoc like abortions, teenage pregnancy, venereal disease, and potential matrimonial disharmony. Sex excites every normal human. You can only enjoy sex in an atmosphere of true and committed marital love. Sex is like having a special birthday celebration

Sex as joyful event

Sex gets everybody's attention. Sex is one of the areas of life that has the most pleasurable information attached to it. We are told we are bad and behave abnormally if we want sex. We cheat if we don't have enough sex. Sex is too joyful to explain. People always want to be in their best mood, dressed well, and wear sweet body scent when they have date. They just want to be alone, eat, drink, kiss, and make love.

SEX PRESENTATION

Sex presentation simply means the packaging and the delivery of sex to your partner or spouse. This area is very sensitive; it can make a marriage or love relationship lovely and intimate, or destroy a relationship and marriage quickly.

There are a number of things you need to know and put in their proper place before you meet your spouse for sex. They are 1) cleanliness of your body, 2) clean and perfumed armpit, 3) sweet breath, 4) sharp tongue, 5) well washed and perfumed vagina and anus, 6) clean cut and perfumed male organ. If you want spontaneous response, good spirit and rational contribution in the sex, all aforementioned conditions must be put in order.

Cleanliness of the body

Your body must be clean and scented with pleasant fragrance. It does not matter how long you have been together or how long a couple has married. What matters is that you are a clean person and your spouse can be comfortable with you. Cleanliness is next to godliness. Your appearance each night to bed must be unique, sweet, and appealing. This is where you have to show your spouse that you are a model and living for him or her.

Clean and perfumed armpit

Some people are unkempt and dirty, with very offensive armpit. This is repulsive to both sexes. Keep your armpits clean, even if your partner does not complain. Make him or her feels like he just found you.

Sweet breath

Nothing is as bad as wanting to kiss a spouse who has offensive and irritating breath. When this happens, your appetite for sex drops. Nobody enjoys making love to someone with bad breath; you will not be able to yield your mind and kiss with such partner. Bad breath irritates sex.

Sharp tongue

Some people keep their tongue cold and like sleep black snow (tongue draws like cold okra soup). This is nasty. You must brush your tongue until it is red clean and sharp. Then your saliva becomes fresh and sweet, kissing continues and is long lasting and enhances your desire. If your partner kisses you once and never want it again, know that something is wrong with your tongue or breathe. Do something about this before you move on to sex

Well washed and perfumed vagina

Some women think the vagina takes care of itself, but that is a wrong idea. You have to take care of it as you take care of your face because that is the final destination of the love journey. An offensive vagina is a disgrace to a woman. The cleaner it is the higher a woman is valued. A decent vagina is a mark of a decent woman and she is every man's choice. Your vagina must be washed at least three times a day with clean water. This diminishes bad scent; it protects the vagina from infections, reduces excessive secretion of vaginal fluid and also gives men who love to suck the desire to do so.

Men should keep private area clean

Like some women, some men keep their private area bushy and dirty, too. Women do not like it. Men have to learn to keep themselves clean, especially for their spouse to be happy and enjoy when sucking them too.

SEX POSITIONS, VARIETY IS THE SPICE OF LIFE

Millions of men around the world cheat on their spouse because of routine sex positions and many women shy away because of the same problem. Human nature is to explore, create, and enjoy; anything short of this is undesirable and uninteresting. Variety in foods makes sense for the balance of one's health. Having sex with different people for variety is dangerous. Woman and men can have variety in a committed relationship by trying different sexual positions.

Each position projects a different image in your mind. Different ideas offer different pleasures and taste. Once you establish variety in your relationship or marriage, you restore the joy of sex and excitement. You enjoy your intimacy.

Men need to understand that women love sex. In fact, some women think about it just as often, if not more, than their male counterparts. Women fantasize constantly and at great length, with men being the object of their desire. These hot little fantasies can cover a broad spectrum of kink, but almost always involve one of the five most common vaginal sex positions women enjoy. This is due to a number of reasons; the most significant is that they create a perfect balance between stage of difficulty and maximum pleasure. In other words, these sex positions women enjoy result in loads of pleasure for the minimal effort required to pull them off. That is not to say that women do not love your favors as well; they are definitely into sexual acrobatics every now and then. When men are getting down and dirty, certain sex positions tend to get women wetter.

HERE ARE SOME OF THE SEX POSITIONS

Missionary position: This is one of the most common sexual positions. The woman lies on her back with her legs extended in front of her body. The man kneels in front of the woman, facing her. Advanced forms of this pose involve the man holding the woman's legs on his shoulders or in the crook of his elbows.

Doggy- style: This is another common sexual position. The woman must pose resting on her hands and knees with her back arched and her rear sticking into the air. The man should be kneeling on the bed behind her, entering her from the rear. This pose can comfortably allow vaginal entry.

The reverse cowgirl: This is a great sexual position that is gaining in popularity. This pose is similar to the missionary position, with the exception of the man on the bottom. In addition, the woman should be facing away from the man, with her rear facing him.

Pig in a Blanket: As the name suggests, you need both a blanket and a pig. Men, being suitably pig-like at times, are designated swine for the outing. Wrap yourselves in a blanket and discreetly wriggle like stuck pigs until you are both satisfied. Save the squealing for later, because there may be people around. Sleeping bags can be used and then you won't have to worry about naked body parts being suddenly exposed to the outside world. The body parts also get nice and sweaty with the friction.

Lumberjack: Simulate sex with a tree in this position. The intermediary is your lover. She is the tree hugger, facing the tree, with her arms around it protecting the tree from your large and violent axe. Enter her from behind, and she will use her otherworldly powers of manipulation to make you forget all about being a callous tree-murderer. Choose your tree carefully, as despite her love for tall leafy greens, she is prejudiced against certain types of trees -- trunks with a lot of scratchy bark are not worthy of her embraces. She likes them long, smooth and thick.

Pitch a Tent: Your throbbing member is the tent peg, and your body is the hammer. She is the ground sheet, flat and spread out, ready for you to make her sturdy and stable with your tools. Peg her to the ground however you need to, and make the most of the ideal position. Once the poles are in, for some variety, she can then make a tent-shape with her body and you can slide the final pole into her satiny fabric -- best done where you would normally pitch a tent.

Bushwhacker: We've all done it, or at least wish we'd done it:

Sex in the bushes reminds us of our misspent youth, curfews, and naughtiness. You don't even have to leave your property – But feel free to do it anywhere. She doesn't want to get her clothes dirty or touch the icky ground, so be a gentleman and kneel at her service. Wrap her legs tightly around your waist, and hold her close so she doesn't have to touch the undergrowth. This way you get the twigs and leaves in your knees and shins as you should, and she gets to have good sex and be treated like the lady she is.

Taking out the Trash: Men are infamous for shirking their domestic duties, so take an opportunity to redeem yourself: Take out the trash, and get her off while you are at it. Yes, sometimes you probably want to send her off with the dump truck, but this time you are going to make passionate love to the garbage bag - her. The connotations are wrong -- she is the furthest thing from trash that exists in the entire world -- but you get the idea. She is wrapped around your upper torso and you carry her like you might carry a large, beautiful sack of rubbish. Enter her body, and revel in the scent of her that is so unlike discarded waste products.

There are many more sex positions to explore and you and your partner can create more that soothe and comfort you. Please, please be creative and enjoy your life and sex with your spouse.

Some Areas to Reform for the Sake of Sweet Marriage

- **Your social life**
- **Your gender difference**
- **Career preference**

Social life

Life has changed a great deal. Men and women have upgraded their lifestyles so much, that they are like a social network: Facebook, Hi5, net-log, MySpace, etc. In love relationships, know that there is jealousy and ownership and no spouse can bear to live such a freelance lifestyle, it hurts. Spouses must be reserved and give their marriage privacy, respect, and regard. Minimize your friendships and coordinate your public affairs in a corporate manner so that people will know and recognize you are married and a responsible person. This is the highest honor you can give to your spouse.

You are a man and a woman of the people, yes, but you must have limits and reserve the best of your social life and privacy for your spouse. No woman wants a spouse who flirts and floats with members of the opposite sex. Neither do men. Once you are married, your life becomes your spouse's life, your network is simply him or her and your spouse must have access to your Facebook page and e-mail Inbox freely. You must be open and hide nothing from your spouse and this makes your marriage or relationship strong and unshakeable.

Your gender difference

Let every man and woman know this: By the divine law of God, by the virtue of creation and standard of nature, man is the head of a family unit. No matter how big a woman is, no matter how educated a woman is, no matter how great is her earning power, she is just but an assistant or subordinate to a man. Two captains cannot be in charge of a ship or should a captain relinquish leadership rights to his assistant, or he will have no legal right to be in that ship. No matter how small a man is, he is a man and must be regarded as such. No matter how weak a man is, he is the head, no matter how little is his earning power, he is the head of the family. Any man who does not take control of his family affairs and cannot provide for his family is worse than an infidel and unqualified for marriage. When you have the knowledge of marriage right and give honor to whom honor is due, you are bound to succeed. Like Esau, men these days have sold their birthright to women, because men are lazy and do not accept responsibility for living a meaningful life. This is shameful and also a curse.

Let the difference be known and each of you take your rightful position in your marriage. Men must do the work of men in the house and women do their house-keeping and child care, but help each other when the need arises. Love is sweet and enjoyable. When you and your spouse work according to God's standard, you will never have issues to divorce.

Career preference

Many people pray day and night, asking God for a partner or a spouse. As we all know, God is kind and gives willingly. Not far from wedlock, spouses no longer have time for each other and devote and commit all their time to their career. This is serious because silence and loneliness will definitely take over their home. It is quite obvious that not every person can stand a lonely life. It drives some people crazy and they will do everything possible to come out of it. A wife must know that her career is also for her husband. She must not starve her spouse of intimacy for a career purpose. Likewise, men should know their success is for their spouse too. They should be able to administer love and intimacy to her for her happiness and health too. Career chase has sent too many good couples into divorce because they no longer feel for each other emotionally and are spiritually disconnected. This situation could result in extra-marital affairs. It is evil and dangerous to your marriage. Upgrade your knowledge and skills, but in such a manner that it does not affect your intimacy with your spouse. If you allow your spouse to discover something different and enjoyable somewhere else, your marriage will have a crack that may widen to break. Too much distance, too long silence, too long malice, and too much career attention are all detrimental to marriage or love relationships.

TIPS ON WHAT SPOUSE SHOULD DO TO ENRICH THEIR SEXUAL FULFILMENT

Both spouses must always take multivitamins (B-Complex, B-12, Folic Acid, etc.). These help to balance the nutrients the body needs to function properly.

Eat fresh food: Most of the foods we eat in the city are dead foods that have stayed too long in the refrigerator. All the nutrients in them are dead and unable to enrich the body. Eat fresh food from the farm within one week of harvest. Eat a lot of fruits and drink fluids.

Eat a mixture of bread, half-boiled eggs, and honey, as often as you can. This mixture enhances sperm production for men.

Make sure your body is not consuming too much sugar, Eat bitter food at least once a month. Example: **Bitter cola, bitter leave, attu- bitters** and so on…Eating bitter food is good for reducing sugar content in the body and detoxifying the liver. It also strengthens men sexual performances.

Drink milk often, and take little wine regularly. This helps in increasing sperm volume in men.

Eat raw sweet-cassava, raw peanuts, and a lot of vegetables and fish. Raw sweet cassava and raw peanuts also enhance sperm count.

Sexual satisfaction is one of the key factors that make a relationship more enjoyable and fulfilling. Although there are other aspects that make or break a relationship, realistically speaking, sexual fulfillment is one of the top considerations. In addition to sexual gratification, having a tight and clean vagina contributes to a woman's respect and sense of wellness.

Some women have a problem of loose vagina walls or opening. This oftentimes creates a lack of sensation when having sexual intercourse which frustrates women. There are a lot ways to tighten your vagina and bring back the fire in your seemingly dormant sexual relationship with your spouse.

HEALTH IMPORTANCE OF THE FOLLOWING FOOD ITEMS

GARCINA KOLA

(Bitter Cola)

Garcina Kola is popularly known as Bitter Kola by the people of West Africa. Bitter Kola is found in the forest and it grows as a medium tree. It is grown domestically and as a cash crop. People in West African region eat Bitter Kola daily, especially the adult men.

Elderly people in Nigeria use Bitter Kola for indigestion. It is also used as an anti-biotic for the treatment of sore, sore throat, chest colds, and cough. In addition it used for the treatment of liver disorders, diabetes, hepatitis, and stomach conditions.

The tree is very common in Nigeria, Ghana, Guinea, Cameroon, Benin, and many other African countries. Bitter Kola is bitter in taste

VERNONIA AMYDALINA

(Bitter Leave)

Vernonia Amydalina, commonly known as bitter leave, it is green plan that grows anywhere in Africa. Bitter leave is a vegetable eaten in Africa but it has medicinal purposes as well. Bitter leave helps improve function of body organs like the kidney and liver. It is also used as a laxative and treatment for malaria. It reduces sugar levels within the body beneficial for those with diabetes and for males it is the "African Viagra"; like bitter cola it is also bitter in taste.

MORE INFORMATION ABOUT A LOOSE VAGINA

For a man to discover their partner has a loose vagina causes shame for women in many countries. A loose vagina prevents both partners from enjoying sex, causing limited sexual pleasure. Women in many countries do what they can to maintain and ensure that their vagina is tight.

There are many factors that contribute to loose vagina i.e. giving birth to over-weight babies, giving birth every nine months, excessive sexual activity, different sizes of male organs, and infection.

How to know one has a loose vagina

For men, it is easy to notice a loose vagina. When a man no longer feel close grip on him inside the vagina, when the man's organ slips out easily and thrusts into the vagina easily, and when he loses pleasure despite of his steady thrusts. Absence of sensation during sexual intercourse for women as well as incontinence are some symptoms of loose vagina.

What can one do about loose vagina?

Kegel exercise: This is one of the most well-known exercises that help tighten the walls of the vagina. Find out how kegel exercise is done and do it regularly. Reducing the amount of fatty foods consumed and eating bitter foods will help tone vaginal walls. Surgery to tighten the vagina is also an option.

What Some African Women do to Tighten Their Vaginal Walls

Some women in Africa do the following when they discover that they have loose vagina:

Luke-warm Water

Women use luke warm water to wash, douche their vagina three or more times a day. This is said to be very beneficial.

Walnut Leaves

Women in Africa use walnut leaves in the treatment of loose vagina and swear by it. Although walnut leaves have documented healing properties for other disorders, such as treating vaginal infections, balancing sugar levels, or as an astringent, there are no documented studies that suggest that Walnut leaves aid in the tightening of the vagina.

Benefits of Tightening Your Vagina

A tighter vagina will help you and your partner enjoy sex more. A tighter vagina actually makes a woman feel more confident and decent. When a woman has a tighter vagina and she and her partner are satisfied sexually, stress levels actually go down.

Chapter 15
APOLOGIES AND RECONCILIATION

In this world, saying "I am sorry" is the only way that one can calm a volcano. As simple as this phrase is, many people do not want to say it because of pride, arrogance, or narrow-mindedness. There are endless wars and conflicts all over the world today because people can neither accept nor say those words...

When it comes to apologizing, people have much to say about it. Businesses "offer" apologies. Situations "lead" to apologies. Celebrities and politicians sometimes "issue" apologies. Some folks "demand" an apology while others "give" an apology. Saying one is "sorry" restores peace and unity.

If you have an inkling or heartfelt conviction that you owe someone an apology, do not put it off. Apologizing right away gives you joy and peace in your life.

An apology in your marriage is more than saying "I am sorry." An apology is an attempt to admit you made a mistake, hurt someone's feelings, did something really stupid, and made a bad decision, and so on. When you apologize, you are accepting responsibility. Trying to justify or rationalize the error is not truly apologizing.

Some people apologize because they just want to get out of the fix they are in or because they want to present a caring and repentant image to others. Focusing on your own needs when you apologize is not really apologizing. Other people apologize because they want to put the past behind them and begin again. Many folks apologize because they are genuinely sorry for what happened, want to accept responsibility for their actions, and want to make amends.

Hopefully, when you apologize to your spouse, it will be because you want to help ease and eventually end any hurt and pain that you caused. Because you love your spouse, you want to do what you can to insure that your marriage is on solid ground. These are excellent reasons to apologize. Do not let friends or family members deceive you into thinking an apology is not necessary. You are the one in the relationship and can feel the heat of differences. An apology can return your sweet relationship with your spouse, your peace, and your progress and confidence for the future.

I think an apology between a husband and wife should be private. When you apologize to your spouse, your apology needs to be genuine and sincere. Use "I" in your apology and don't try to put any responsibility for your behavior on your spouse. If you have extended the matter to your family unit or mentor, then you must apologize in their presence. Let your spouse know that because they have been involved and must also be involved in the settlement.

Although humor may have worked for your spouse, don't try to be funny during an apology. Keep your apology on target. Don't ramble.

Apologizing in the form of a letter is acceptable. However, if possible, you should be present when the letter is read by your spouse. Express your shame, regret, sadness, guilt, and so on. You also need to state what you are willing to do to make things right again. Some spouses apologize by giving a gift and quickly saying, "I am sorry I hurt you, darling," and from this point, dialogue starts. Some spouses arrange lunch or dinner somewhere and sincerely apologize at the meal.

An apology should emphasize one's determination to not make the same mistake again. Whatever the restitution, make sure it is meaningful and something that you will do. Don't make promises you will not or cannot keep. Finally, you need to ask for forgiveness. Don't push your spouse for an immediate response. Your spouse may need time to respond. Do not forget to forgive yourself too.

RECONCILIATION IN MARRIAGE

Forgiveness is a key factor in the reconciliation process... "Forgiveness is giving up your desire to see that the other person is not punished in any form. Un-forgiveness is the poison you offer to somebody else but its bitterness hurts you instead. Reconciliation, on the other hand, replaces hostility and separation with peace and friendship. It is admitting failures and mistakes, and being willing to consider and offer changes in attitudes and behaviors that contribute to conflict in a marriage.

During the reconciliation process, couples should demonstrate their willingness to look at their individual failures and mistakes in the relationship. Each of them have to be open to change.

In the reconciliation process, the most important insight to understand is that you can't control another person. The only person you can control is yourself, so your focus has to be on how you can improve the relationship, how you can do unto your spouse what you would want to be done unto you.

Couples should focus on attacking the problem; not each other. The goal should be to win your spouse over, not win over him or her. This does not equal reconciliation; it just creates more hostility and separation.

TIPS FOR RECONCILIATION IN A MARRIAGE

First, think about specific attitudes and behaviors you are doing that contribute to the conflict.

Second, admit those attitudes and actions to your spouse at an appropriate time. This is not a talk you want to have when you are both tired and hungry. Third, is to apologize: "in this I was wrong, sweetheart. I am sorry. Please forgive me. I love you."

Search for creative solutions that will improve your relationship. We generally try to solve the problem before we fully understand it (we get the tip of the iceberg and run with it). Try hard to understand the other person's point of view. At this point, listening becomes more important than speaking. Listen until each person feels understood. By doing this, you stand a much greater chance of solving the problem and moving the relationship forward.

In order for a marriage to work, you must communicate. You have to talk about the little things that cause disagreement so that those little things do not become big things.

Marriage is a lifelong union and you have to handle it with knowledge. You cannot afford to change life partners like paper plates. Marriage means much more than that. There is no perfect partner out there, but together you can build a relationship to please both of you.

WHAT THE BIBLE SAYS ABOUT MARRIAGE

Marriage is a "divine institution." Contrary to contemporary opinion; marriage is not a human institution that has evolved over the millennia to meet the needs of society. If it were no more than that, then conceivably it could be discarded when it is deemed no longer to be meeting those needs. Rather marriage is God's idea, and human history begins with the Lord Himself presiding over the first marriage. (Genesis 2:18-25)

Marriage is to be regulated by "divine law" Since God made marriage; it stands to reason that it must be regulated by His commands. In marriage, both husband and wife stand beneath the authority of the Lord. Unless the Lord builds the house, you labor in vain who build the house. (Psalm 127:1)

Marriage is a divine law in both the Old and the New Testaments.

Marriage is used as the supreme illustration of the love relationship that God established with His people.

Israel is spoken of as the wife of Jehovah (Isaiah 54:5; Jeremiah 3:8; Hosea 2:19-20). The Church is called the bride of Christ (Ephesians 5:22-32).

It can be said that the Christian marriage is sort of a "pageant" in which the husband takes the part of the Lord Jesus, loving and leading his wife as Christ does the Church; and the wife plays the role of the believer, loving and submitting to her husband as the Christian does to the Lord.

Thus Christian marriage should be a reflection in which others can see something of the divine-human relationship.

Marriage is a "covenant." From the earliest chapters of the Bible, the idea of a covenant is the framework by which man's relationship to God is to be understood, and which also regulates the lives of God's people. A covenant is an agreement between two parties, based upon mutual promises and solemnly binding obligations. It is like a contract, with the additional idea that it establishes personal relationships. God's covenant with Abraham and his descendants is summarized in the statement, I will be your God, and you shall be my people.

Marriage is called a covenant (Malachi 2:14), the most intimate of all human covenants. The key ingredient in a covenant is faithfulness, being committed irreversibly to the fulfillment of the covenant obligations. The most important factor in the marriage covenant is not romance; it is faithfulness to the covenant vows, even if the romance flickers. (Till death do us part).

Marriage is a "whole person commitment." God meant marriage to be the total commitment of a man and woman to each other. It is not two solo performances, but a duet. In marriage, two people give themselves unreservedly to each other (Genesis 2:25; 1 Corinthians 7:3,4).

"What God has joined together, let no man separate," declared our Lord (Matthew 19:6) is not a carry-over from old-fashioned romanticism, but a sober reflection of God's intention regarding marriage (Romans 7:2, 3; 1 Corinthians 7:39).

WHAT THE BIBLE TEACHES ABOUT DIVORCE

Jesus said, "It was because of the hardness of your heart that made Moses gave the certificate of divorce; in the beginning it was not so." (Mathew 19:8)

Divorce is abhorrent to God (Malachi 2:15, 16) Divorce is always the result of sin. God's basic intention for marriage never included divorce. Single people commit fornication and married people commit adultery. When you are on courtship, if you discover that your spouse-to-be is sexually immoral, then you divorce the marriage plan. This was the case between Joseph and the Virgin Mary. They were not married and never had any sex but Joseph discovered that she was pregnant and planned to divorce the idea of marrying her.

HOW MANY TIMES WOULD YOUR BROTHER, YOUR WIFE, AND YOUR HUSBAND SIN AGAINST YOU BEFORE YOU HOLD IT AGAINST HIM OR HER? (MATHEW 18: 21-22) We have to forgive a partner 490 times before complaint. This means exercising unlimited amount of forgiveness, so there is no allowance for divorce.

CONCLUSION

Our society today is sitting on a time bomb of liberty and lawlessness. Every one of us has wandered very far away from God, even though we say, "In God we trust." We are individually, in a collective dimension, building a tower of our own destruction. Everything that the Lord prohibits, we desire and adore. With our hands, we dismantle every structure God has made for our good; and with pride, we parade before Him in disobedience and in wickedness. Lord, please have mercy and please put in us a new heart and spirit of love for you and our fellow brethren.

Friendship, relationship, and marriage; especially marriage; are all issues of the heart. Anything that affects the heart of a man affects the entire body, which undoubtedly affects the society. Human hearts must be guided in all area of human endeavor and in particular marriage, before getting into it. Shady knowledge and wrong assumptions will permanently destroy us and any generation that would come. So many people always dream for a perfect partner, knowing deep down in their hearts that they are not perfect themselves. Making a description of your dream partner in life is like searching the sky for a star on snowy day. This is a complete illusion, it cannot be found but you can form one. Two imperfect people come together to build perfection; it is a hard task. No wonder the

Lord said, "before building a house, you must first sit down and cost it." You must make sure you are strong enough to take on the project, because it makes no sense to start building and stop halfway. That means an abandoned project; you cannot go further, and the money you could have used to do something else is wasted. You lost everything, and especially your value. People will laugh at you. When imperfection tries to build perfection, there must be a lot tolerance, a lot of giving, a lot of accepting, a lot of disagreeing to agree, a lot of quarreling (but not fighting), and a lot of forgiveness. Above all, you must have LOVE, the kind of love that you have for yourself and where the Lord Himself can show up in your marriage. Love is the most powerful energy in Heaven and on Earth. Love does no evil, no matter what happens. Love does not keep record of offenses and mistakes, or settle scores in any form. Love is endless and selfless in generosity.

Do not ever go into marriage for material things. Never allow your relationship and marriage to stand on something other than love, because when that starts to disappoint or fade, your marriage starts to fade too. Love is the only being who never disappoints or fades. I am not saying here that things will not go wrong. Some bad things may happen. You may fight, you may curse each other and do some other funny things, but because there is love, you both will never fall apart. Love is a great repairer of wrongs and love can cement broken hearts, so it will seem like nothing bad ever happened.

Nobody wants to be hurt but a life in solitary confinement is lonely and dull. God knows you need somebody to scratch your head and scrub your back for you. This is why God made them males and females. Children should know a home and be part of a family unit and be cared for by both parents, many children who would have been great personalities in this society have killed themselves out of frustration; many have joined bad gangs to have a sense of belonging, and many are facing health disaster because of divorce.

It does not matter how long your marriage has soured or seemed dead, you can repair it if you are willing. It does not matter how long you have been divorced and you have not remarried. Use the teachings in this book, to bring back your spouse and your love. Marriage will be sweet this time and last for life. Remember, your children, need both parents. Remember, there is no dignity in divorce.

Commit your marriage, body, and soul to your God, the author and finisher of our faith. Commit to Him in prayers of righteousness and in holiness so your marriage will be secured and safe forever and ever.

BIBLIOGRAPHY

Ali, A. Y. (2011). *The Holy Quran*. Rockville, MD: Solomon Publishing.

Elliott, J. (2005, November 30). *How Does Religion Affect the Lives of Adolescents*. Retrieved from Yahoo Voices: Mental Health: http://voices.yahoo.com/how-does-religion-affect-lives-adolescents-11697.html

Marx, K. (2002). *Karl Marx on Religion*. Philadelphia, PA: Temple University Press.

Terry Ellis & Jerry Rockwell. (2008). *The Rock of Ages Study Bible KJV*. Cleveland, TN: Rock of Ages Press.

Woodhead, L. (2001). *Peter Berger and the Study of Religion*. London; New Yourk: Routledge.

ABOUT THE AUTHOR

Apostle Felix Jeremiah has an undergraduate degree in theology and business, a Master degree in psychology, and working toward his PhD in ministry. Born and raised in Nigeria, he now resides in the USA. Apostle Jeremiah aspires to encourage understanding of God's plan for their lives, love and relationships.

CPSIA information can be obtained at www.ICGtesting.com
Printed in the USA
LVOW08s0715250913

353947LV00001B/70/P

9 781452 577708